A Complicated
Heart

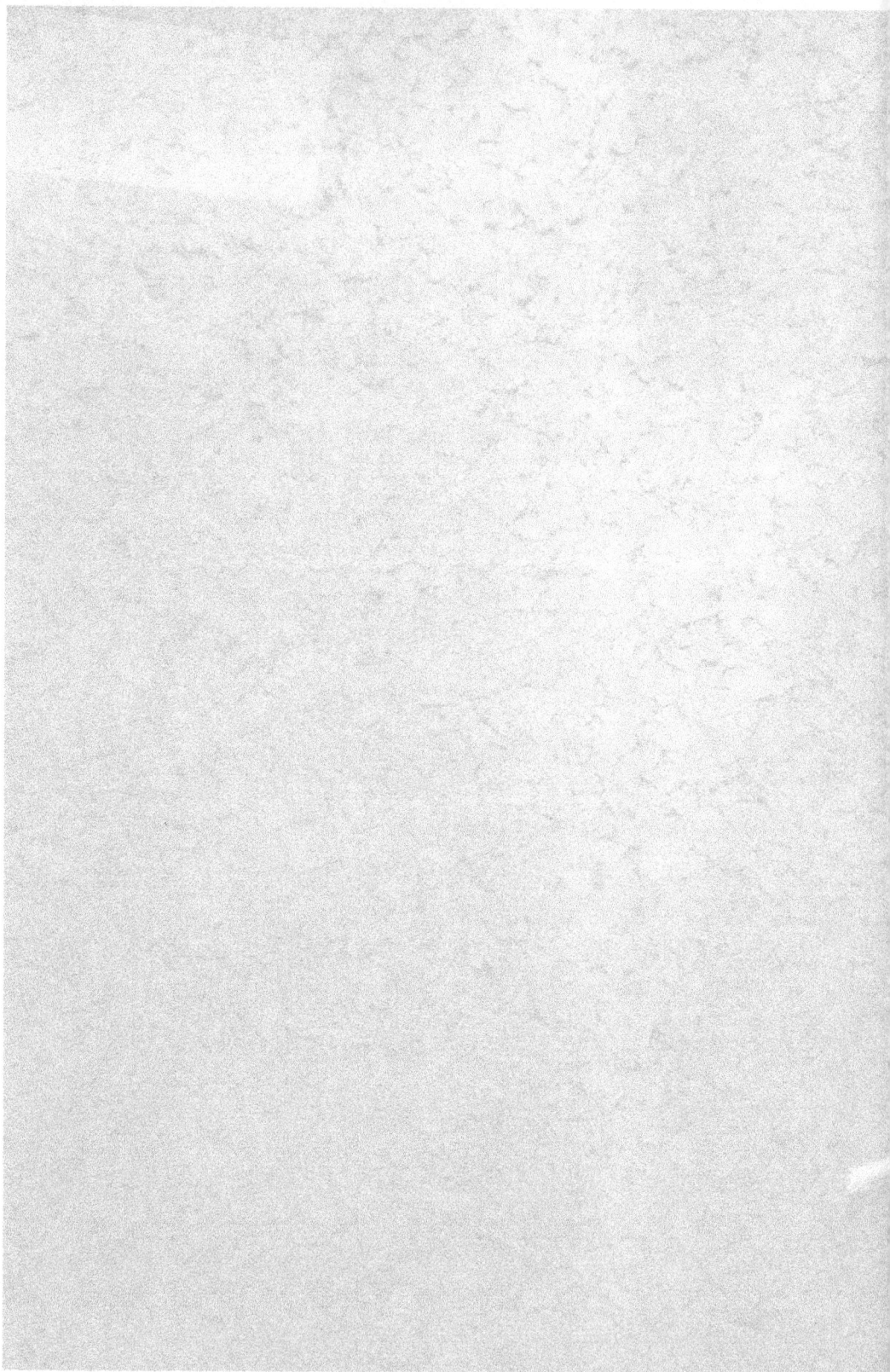

A Complicated
Heart

How Working as a Judge,
Lawyer, and Midwife
Taught Me What Really Matters

Sheri A. Raphaelson

SUNSTONE
PRESS

SANTA FE

Sunstone books may be purchased for educational, business, or sales promotional use.
For information please write: Special Markets Department, Sunstone Press,
P.O. Box 2321, Santa Fe, New Mexico 87504-2321.

Book and Cover design › Vicki Ahl
Body typeface › Adobe Caslon Pro
Printed on acid-free paper
∞

Library of Congress Cataloging-in-Publication Data

Raphaelson, Sheri A.
  A complicated heart : how working as a judge, lawyer, and midwife taught me what
really matters / by Sheri A. Raphaelson.
      p. cm.
  ISBN 978-0-86534-922-3 (softcover : alk. paper)
  1. Raphaelson, Sheri A. 2. United States. District Court (New Mexico)--Biography.
3. Judges--New Mexico--Biography. I. Title.
  KF373.R37R37 2012
  347.73'22092--dc23
  [B]
                                    2012041440

WWW.SUNSTONEPRESS.COM
SUNSTONE PRESS / POST OFFICE BOX 2321 / SANTA FE, NM 87504-2321 /USA
(505) 988-4418 / ORDERS ONLY (800) 243-5644 / FAX (505) 988-1025

To my parents,
Howard Raphaelson and Alice Koval Raphaelson.
They have been with me from the beginning.

1

Thank You for Saving My Life

The large conference room table was full. The head Drug Court probation officer, two regular probation officers, a family therapist, an addiction counselor, my secretary, my bailiff, and at the head of the table, me; the judge. We were organizing our papers getting ready to start the meeting. The meeting where I hear reports on how well all the Drug Court participants are cooperating with their treatment so I can decide who continues to get rewarded and who goes to jail.

"Judge, your boyfriend is in jail again." The probation officer teased. She had a devious half smile on her face.

"Who?" I have certainly had Drug Court participants whom I felt had a strong chance to succeed, my favorites of the criminals, but I couldn't think of anyone currently in the program. Lately I've had a soft spot for Eli Acosta. High hopes for his success. But he's not in Drug Court, just on regular probation.

Must be Eli. Please don't be Eli. I know she means Eli. He must have broken the rules. Maybe something minor. He left the County without permission? He moved without giving his probation officer his new address? He was socializing with another person on probation? The worst would be that he got arrested for committing a new crime, but there were a lot of possibilities that didn't spell certain failure.

"You aren't talking about Eli Acosta are you?" I asked quietly, not wanting to hear the answer. She shook her head.

"What did he do?" My eyes were down at the table hoping if I didn't look at her when she said it somehow it wouldn't be true.

"Failure to report to the probation office, and alcohol consumption."

"No heroin? He wasn't using heroin?" I asked hopefully.

"We didn't catch him with it, but that doesn't mean anything. We went to do a home visit at another probationer's house and he was there drinking. The probationer wasn't even there. Eli was drinking with the guy's sister."

Not as bad as it could be, but not great either. If he was drinking, he was probably drugging too.

The first time I met Eli was when he was in my court for arraignment. He had been indicted for cocaine possession. He had waited quietly on one of the wooden benches in the audience until I called his case close to the end of the long morning list. When he walked up to the front of the courtroom, his public defender waiting there for him, he swayed a little. If I wasn't in criminal court I would have just thought he was tired. But nodding off like just before falling asleep is the classic look of someone on heroin.

I turn to the page in my script book that contains the advisement of rights for a first appearance.

Me: "Sir, has your attorney told you what you're charged with?"

Eli: "Yeah."

Me: "Has your attorney told you the minimum and maximum possible penalties for the crime you're charged with?"

Eli: "Yeah."

Me: "Do you have any questions about the possible penalties?"

Eli: "Yeah."

Me: "What is it you want to know about the penalties?"

Eli: (Long pause) "Yes sir" he says slowly and inappropriately. His lawyer whispers in his ear "I mean yes Ma'am."

I can tell he's high on something. I continue.

Me: "You have the right to a trial by jury. That means twelve people from the community would listen to the evidence in your case and determine if you are guilty or not guilty. The State has the burden of proving you are guilty beyond a reasonable doubt. You do not have to prove that you are innocent. Do you understand your right to a trial by jury and the burden of proof?"

Eli: "I'm having a trial now?" His speech is slow.

Me: "No Sir. This is the very beginning of your case. A trial would happen much later." His lawyer is trying to get him to stop talking, but Eli's ignoring him.

Eli: "I want a lawyer." A little chuckle from the audience.

Me: "Your lawyer is standing right next to you Sir."

I finish advising him of his rights and his lawyer says "not-guilty." Now I'm going to set his bond. Normally someone who shows up to court voluntarily I will let out without a bond, expecting them to keep showing up to their hearings in the future. But if he's come to court on drugs, I'm not so sure I want to give him the benefit of the doubt.

Me: "Sir it looks to me like you're high right now. Are you high?"

Eli looks at me and starts slowly shaking his head no, his lawyer is telling him not to say anything. Eli is looking between his lawyer and me and seems overwhelmed with the relatively action-less action.

Me: "Sir, the reason I'm asking is that I want you to be able to understand what's going on here. This is important. If you aren't up to this now I can put off the rest of the hearing until the afternoon when you may be able to pay attention better." Now I need to remind him and everyone else in the courtroom that I'm the one with the power. When a woman is on the bench, and being polite, it's easy for people to forget who's in charge.

"And also, if you come to court high, it's contempt. You can't do that. Well, I guess what I mean to say is that you *can* do that, but you *shouldn't* do that. I can put you in jail for that."

Eli: "I'm not high. I just have a bad tooth ache and I didn't sleep last night." Here's the classic addict lie: I have a legitimate condition that requires pain medication. The set up is the tooth ache and he will get to the Percoset or Valium or some other drug that he took for the pain. He will leave out the part that he didn't have a prescription and bought it on the street. And then when I tell him he looks like he's on more than just one Valium from last night, he'll say that he took some Nyquil too and that really made him tired and that's probably why he looks so bad. If I keep pushing he'll eventually say he also had some alcohol, and then it was a Codeine in the morning, but that was a mistake because his friend gave it to him and he thought it was just Tylenol but his friend actually gave him a Tylenol-Codeine (don't you just hate when that happens) but he didn't know that until after he took it. He will desperately add more and more layers to the lie until it is a giant swirled lollipop with the red, bright green and yellow of the coils all running into each other. No matter how convoluted or improbable the tale gets, he will never admit the truth: he's a heroin addict and used before he came to court.

Me: "Well Sir, I would like you to go across the street to the jail and take a drug test. If it comes back clean, I'll let you go home. If it comes out dirty, then I'm probably going to set a bond for you and you may end up staying in jail."

Eli: "I'm clean. I promise. I'll take a test 'cause I'm clean."

I motion to the Deputy who takes Eli by the arm and leads him out of the courtroom.

I have plenty more cases to hear and quickly forget about Eli. I am finishing with the last of the morning hearings when the Deputy comes back into the courtroom. When I have excused the final defendant, and the public defender and the prosecutor are clearing their files from their respective tables, the Deputy comes up to my bailiff and they talk quickly.

I am piling up my papers to give to my secretary and my bailiff comes over and tells me to wait.

"He wants to talk to you." My bailiff whispers to me from across the bench.

"Who?"

"Eli, the drug test guy. The Deputy says he wants to talk to you."

"One more case" I announce loudly to the lawyers just before they walk away from their tables and head out for the lunch break. "We're going to go back on the record in State of New Mexico versus Eli, uh," I look to my right at the court monitor sitting behind recording machines as I try to remember his last name. She looks down at her papers and whispers 'Acosta.' "-Acosta" I say.

The Deputy steps closer to the bench and my bailiff shakes his head 'no' and then says "not on the record, he wants to talk to you alone" then he laughs a little. Obviously that's not how things are done.

I look to the Deputy. "I have him back in the jury room. He told me that he wants to talk to you alone."

"About what? I can't talk to him about his case unless the lawyers are there. Was he dirty?"

"He said he couldn't give a sample. I knew it wasn't true and I told him we would come back here and I would tell you he refused to give a sample. On the way back he admitted that he would come out dirty, but he said he wanted to talk to you about it. Alone." The Deputy paused and glanced around. The only people still in the courtroom were the two attorneys, who were standing still and listening, my bailiff, and my court monitor. Quietly the Deputy says "he's crying."

"He's crying?" I repeat, intrigued.

The Deputy shakes his head, kind of embarrassed for Eli.

This was just strange enough that I wanted to know more. I turn to my court monitor and slice my hand across the air indicating that she can go off the record. My bailiff knows that I'm about to break every rule of safety and sit in the small jury room with a criminal defendant. He shoots me a look but knows that I'm going to do it anyway.

"Let's go." I walk off the bench, through the empty rows of seats in the audience and to the door of the jury room in the back corner of the courtroom, the echoing sound of my heels clicking on the wood floor muffled slightly as the bottom of my black robe ripples around my legs. My bailiff and the Deputy follow me. I didn't need a whole hour to eat lunch anyway.

Eli was sitting at the jury table and another Deputy was standing behind him. Eli was looking down at the big table. His face would have been in his hands, but they were cuffed together and chained around his waist. When I walked in he slowly turned his head towards me. We looked at each other, only a few feet apart in awkward silence. One of the Deputies told Eli to rise, unsure of the proper protocol.

The jury room was just big enough for the large conference table and the twelve chairs that surrounded it. This was a tight space. Me and Eli sort of in the middle, and the Deputies and my bailiff encircling us.

"The Deputy said you wanted to talk to me. So what did you want to tell me?"

Eli motioned his head to my bailiff directly behind me and the Deputy closest to him "Can't they leave" he quietly asked.

My bailiff answered for me "If she's here, I'm here." His hand on his tazer. I know it made him nervous to have me in this situation.

Eli stumbled. "Well, I have to tell you something but I just don't want to say it in front of everyone." He looked to the Deputy behind him. "Can he leave?"

The two Deputies and my bailiff exchanged glances. I looked at them, making it clear with my expression I would like it to happen if it could, but it was their decision. They nodded. The one Deputy left the room. The remaining Deputy and my bailiff could handle a cuffed Eli if he got out of control.

I unzipped my robe, sat down at the table next to the chair Eli had been sitting in, and invited him to sit down again. I hoped he would be comfortable enough to talk.

He put his head down, embarrassed, and started.

"I lied to you. I shouldn't have, but I did. I did use last night. I took a perc. My tooth was killing me. I just took one."

Me: "No you didn't. You're higher than that." (Eli looked away from me.) "You took one, I believe that, but then you did a lot more. No one comes to court high on purpose. You know you're going to get in trouble. You'd never do it if you could help it. You used because you couldn't control yourself. You're an addict. You didn't choose to use, you couldn't help it."

Eli: "I took the perc but my tooth was still hurting so I had some whiskey too. It must have been the two together. I swear, it was the one pill and the whiskey."

Me: "And what else? You're already in trouble. I know you're high. Just tell me what else. I want to help you. I really do. I can only help you if you're honest with me. Look, you wanted to talk to me in private and here I am. I wouldn't be here like this if I didn't want to help you. Just tell me the truth. It doesn't matter what you took, but it matters that you be honest about it."

Eli: "I wasn't always like this. I never wanted to be like this. I'm so embarrassed. You see my parents died over a year ago. I was really close to them and then they died in a car wreck. I used to be okay before that. I mean I used some, mostly drinking, but I was okay. And now since they died its gotten worse. I don't have anywhere to go. I was living with them. I've stolen from everyone else. No one trusts me anymore. I have one aunt and she's tried to help but she's far away. I can't believe I'm crying. I didn't used to be this bad. I've gotten really bad."

Me: "If you want help I'll let you get help. The only way you're going to get clean is if you're ready to. I could order you to go to treatment but it won't work unless you're ready for it. Some people are never ready."

Eli: "I want treatment. I don't want to be like this. Please don't send me to jail, send me to treatment. I'll go wherever you want. Don't put me in jail. I can't go to jail."

Me: "I'm afraid if I release you you're going to get worse. I'll let you go to treatment, but for your own safety I want you in jail. You can start to get clean in jail and then go to treatment. I can arrange for the social worker from the public defender to come talk to you. Figure out what treatment program you can get into."

Eli: "But I can't go to jail. I CAN'T! Please just let me go to treatment."

Me: "You can go to treatment. I'll let you go, but you're going to wait in jail until there's a bed available. That's the compromise. I'll help you get treatment but you have to go there directly from jail."

Eli's hanging his head and shaking it back and forth. He's getting agitated. He's starting to breathe hard enough that I can hear him sucking in air and intentionally letting it out in puffs. The Deputy and my bailiff get a little closer.

Me: "Just stay calm. I promise I'll try to help you. That's why I'm here with you right now. I want to help you."

Eli: "But there's something I have to tell you. You don't understand. Can't you guys leave? I really need to talk to her alone."

Me: "They're not going to leave. You can whisper in my ear."

Eli: "Just take off my cuffs. I have to show her something. Please, just take them off for a minute. You guys will be here the whole time. I'm not gonna do her nothing. I just want to show her. Well then, will you roll up my sleeves? Please, just roll up my sleeves."

We all glance around. No one wants to touch Eli. He's dirty, sweaty, dripping tears, and has been using who knows what. Maybe unhook him from the belly chain, but leave the cuffs on, I suggest. Reluctantly the Deputy obliges. The crying increases and slowly Eli pushes up one sleeve and then the other. He turns his palms up and holds his arms out in front of me. The only sound is his crying. I immediately think of two things: 1) the game I played as a child where you balance a large silver ball on top of two chop-stick like dowels that are joined at one end. You slowly open the sticks wider and wider, rolling the ball as far down them as you can without letting the ball drop through the sticks, and 2) a melon-baller. Eli's arms look like the sticks, and the deep gouges in the flesh look like they were made by a melon-baller.

I have seen stillborn babies, jagged flesh where stitches were ripped open when a drunk husband insisted on having sex the day after his wife gave birth, an autopsy picture of a head with the flesh carefully peeled off, and the exposed bone in my thumb when the ceramic drawer handle shattered in my hand and sliced through my skin, but I have never seen anything like the arms stretched out before me.

The gouges cover the surfaces of both arms. Some deeper than others and all of different ages. Some have dark, bumpy skin across them, having healed completely, and others are pink or red, with new skin stretched across the dips like a loose trampoline top. The skin is wet with sweat, but nothing is coming out of the wounds. My mind is clicking through possibilities and I settle on this; he was shooting up with dirty needles and the injection sites got infected. The infections went untreated, got worse, and the flesh started rotting away. He must have eventually gone to the hospital. I knew a fifteen years old boy on probation, in Drug Court, who had run away from home and was living on the streets. When the police found him weeks later he almost had to have his arms amputated because of out of control infections where he was shooting up heroin.

Eli: "This is why I can't go to jail. I'm sick. I'll die in there. Please don't send me to jail."

He pushes his sleeves back down. He is crying harder. Pleading with me.

Eli: "I don't want to die. Please let me go to treatment. I never used to use heroin. I don't know how I got like this. Don't send me to jail judge. I'm begging you. Please, let me go with my aunt. I'll check in with probation every day. Whatever you want. You can't send me to jail—I'll die!"

Me: "What did you use? What would you test positive for? Be honest."

Eli: "Percoset."

Me: "And."

Eli: "Weed."

Me: "And."

Eli: "Coke."

Me: "And."

Eli: "Heroin."

Me: "And."

Eli: "That's it. I swear."

Me: "Thank you for telling me. For being honest. I know you're a good person. I know that this isn't who you really are. I know that you want to stop using and you can't, that it's stronger than you."

Eli: "So you won't put me in jail? You won't let me die?"

Me: "No. That's exactly why I am putting you in jail. Because I don't want you to die. I know you don't agree with me. I know you don't want to go, but you're still going. I think it's the best way I can help you and that's why I'm doing it."

The Deputy takes hold of Eli's belly chain, careful not to touch his shirt any more than he has to, and starts to turn him towards the door. I stand up from the table and Eli turns to face me and makes one last plea.

Eli: "Please judge, please don't send me to jail! You're gonna kill me!"

Me: "I'm not doing this to punish you. I know it might seem like that, but I'm doing this because I want to help you."

He doesn't believe me. Why would he. His tears are flowing again and he looks at me like I've just tricked him. I know it took a lot for him to tell me what he was on, to admit he was an addict. He shouldn't feel betrayed after that, he should feel relieved. Appreciated. If he was in an AA meeting there would be clapping, but this isn't an AA meeting. He's a criminal defendant and I'm his judge. I do the only thing I can think of to reward him for his courage and prove that I want what's best for him.

I hug him.

I hug all of the disgustingness that everyone else has so carefully been avoiding, including me. He's a good person who has made bad choices. I can see past the dirty clothes and the lunar surface of his arms. I want him to see past that too.

Walking back through the empty courtroom to my office, my bailiff shakes his head in disgust. "I can't believe you touched him."

My thoughts went back four or five years before. When I was still a lawyer and stopped at the store on the way home from my office.

"I know that voice. I would recognize that voice anywhere!" The man's voice came from down the aisle and at first I didn't pay any attention, assuming that he was talking to someone else. I was in the little grocery store between my office and my house. I was standing in front of the refrigerated case looking at cakes.

The German Chocolate cake was my immediate first choice, but we were discussing the small, round double layer fudge cake since it might be more to the liking of my eight year old. This was the kind of grocery store that had been in business before the twenty-four hour supermarkets existed. Five or six aisles total, wooden shelves, very few brands, very few choices, but a meat counter that still has an on-site butcher. If you know to ask, which I do, at the end of the day you can buy a cardboard box full of the scrap bones for your dog. Sometimes it's one dollar, sometimes two depending on who's working the register. I didn't want to do anything special for my forty-third birthday, but my parents were visiting and my mother insisted.

As I was carefully shuffling the plastic cake containers, reading off the names of the cakes to my mother, making sure we knew all of the options before making our choice, a man's voice came from behind me, down the short aisle. "I know that voice, I would recognize that voice anywhere!"

I glanced up and saw we were the only people in the aisle. I then knew he must be talking about me, but I didn't know why. Hesitantly I turned around. I had been a lawyer in this town for fourteen years and represented hundreds, perhaps a thousand people. Most of them happy with the outcome of their cases, but not all of them. When someone recognized me, I never knew which way it was going to go.

This man had a big smile on his face, like he was meeting someone at the airport. I could relax. He was happy with the outcome.

He was probably in his late forties, early fifties. It was December. He wore heavy tan work pants, scuffed boots, and a black leather jacket, half zipped. He probably hadn't been wearing that nice jacket when he was working during the day, but within a half hour of the sun going down, the temperature had taken a quick dive. I didn't recognize him, but that wasn't unusual. He probably had only had one lawyer in his life and easily remembers my face, but I'd had lots of clients.

"You don't remember me do you?"

I was past being embarrassed by this situation. "You look familiar" I would politely lie, "remind me of your name."

"Jose Lucero. You saved me that time in court. I never got to thank you. You saved me!" He was talking excitedly.

"I'm sorry. I just don't exactly remember, but I'm glad everything worked out."

"Worked out? More than worked out!"

Words started spilling from his mouth. As he was talking his hands were moving, his head was shaking, he was looking at me, my mother, and back at me. He was telling a story he had told many times before. It was his story, but I was in it.

As he spoke, the situation he was describing started to float above me like clouds. The more he talked, the lower the clouds got to me. They began to organize themselves. An eraser rubbed itself around the fluffy white edges, revealing a neat penciled line.

He was in Magistrate Court on what I would consider a minor charge: Criminal Damage to Property. Representing himself. Thought it was no big deal, until he got there and realized he could go to jail.

Mr. Lucero went on to tell me that when he was in his court hearing I was sitting in the back of the courtroom. He hadn't even noticed me since he was so nervous about his own situation. The police officer who was prosecuting Mr. Lucero had finished telling the judge everything that Mr. Lucero had done wrong and why he was guilty.

The basic story was that he had an argument with his wife. He thought she was cheating on him with someone from her work. She denied it, but he grabbed her purse and dumped it out on the couch. There was a greeting card that had been put back in the opened envelope. The front of the envelope said "To My Someone Special." He didn't even take the card out. He didn't want to know what it said. There was a picture on the end table next to the couch; Mr. Lucero and his wife standing behind their daughter who was sitting in a chair holding a little baby. The Christmas tree was in the background. It was in a heavy white ceramic frame that had 'Baby's First Christmas' in red script across the top. Mrs. Lucero had bought that frame and another one just like it. One for herself and one for her daughter. They had matching pictures.

Mr. Lucero grabbed the picture, and in a rage, threw it at the wall. The frame gouged the wall and then broke into pieces. Mr. Lucero had never been like this before. His wife dialed 911.

After the officer finished telling the judge what Mrs. Lucero had told him that night, and showed the judge the picture he took of the marred wall and the broken frame on the ground beneath it, Mr. Lucero began explaining.

He suspected the affair had been going on for some time. He had asked but she always denied it. They had problems, like any couple, but nothing major. They had been married twenty-two years. He worked a lot and wasn't home much. He didn't like it either, but they were helping to support their daughter and her baby. The dad wasn't any good. Drank a lot. Mr. Lucero's overtime at the saw mill really helped. He knew he shouldn't have done it, but he just got so mad. The thought of his wife with someone else. He got out of control. You understand judge, don't you?

The police officer told the judge that even if Mr. Lucero had a good reason, even if morally he was in the right, it was a crime to damage someone's property. Mrs. Lucero had bought the frame, and he smashed it into pieces. The confidence with which the uniformed police officer declared the contents of the law, and what acts it would take to violate it, made him very convincing. In Magistrate Court the judges are not lawyers. The cases are minor, except to the person on trial.

The judge was patiently explaining his view of the case to Mr. Lucero. I had been in front of him enough to know that he was letting Mr. Lucero down gently. He was getting to the part of his speech where he would say "so, based on all of the evidence before me, I find you guilty." I wasn't absolutely sure, but it sounded like he might also be sentencing Mr. Lucero to a few days in jail. This would have been very unfortunate.

Despite the police officer's confidence about what the law was, he was wrong. In order to be guilty Mr. Lucero would have had to damage the property of *another*. New Mexico is a community property state. If the picture frame was purchased during the marriage, which it was, then it belonged to Mr. Lucero and his wife equally, regardless of who actually went to the store and bought it. It wasn't against the law for Mr. Lucero to break his *own* property.

I sat in the back of the courtroom trying to tell myself that it wasn't my business. That this wasn't my case. That there are no circumstances when it is proper to interrupt a judge. My only obligation was to the clients that I was representing that day, of which Mr. Lucero was not one.

The judge had announced his guilty verdict and was moving on to sentencing. He talked about fines, how they tend to punish not just the wrong doer, but the whole family. Take food off the table. Gas out of the car. That he didn't want to punish the family here, just Mr. Lucero. This was definitely the you're-going-to-jail-for-the weekend speech. When it was almost over I couldn't bear it anymore.

"Judge" I said loudly. I stood up from my seat in the back of the courtroom "that's not actually the law." The police officer, Mr. Lucero and everyone in the audience waiting for their turn, twisted around to look. The judge leaned a little to one side so he could see me clearly past the podium. He knew me, respected my opinion, and I was the only lawyer in the room.

"What's that Ms. Raphaelson?"

I speak carefully knowing I have broken courtroom etiquette. "Well, the officer has it wrong. Criminal Damage to Property requires that you damage the property of another, not your own property." The officer glares at me. I focus my eyes on the judge. "It doesn't necessarily make a lot of sense" I give the officer the ability to save face, "but that's the way the statute is written. He and the victim are married. Even if she bought the frame, since it was purchased during the marriage, it's community property. It belongs to both of them. Mr. Lucero is an owner, so he can break it if he wants to. You may not like that he did it, but it just isn't against the law." I sit down and slowly the heads turn back around to front of the courtroom.

The judge looks at the officer and raises his substantial gray eyebrows, asking the officer if he has anything to say. The officer looks down.

The judge goes back to addressing Mr. Lucero. "Well, if that's what the law says, then I guess you're not guilty." He writes something on a piece of paper and puts it in the file. "Mr. Lucero, you can pick up your paperwork from the clerk in the lobby. Your case is over. Your bond is released."

As Mr. Lucero was telling me the story I could remember a few details that would have been part of my story, not his.

I remember finally standing up and interrupting when I couldn't take it anymore. I remember the nasty look the officer gave me. How he would have said something to go along with it if the circumstances had been different. I can't remember the other cases I had that day, the cases of my actual clients, but I do remember standing up for Mr. Lucero. Realizing at that moment what "to stand up for someone" really means. I literally stood up for Mr. Lucero. For the law. For justice.

Mr. Lucero was finishing up the story. I could tell he had told it many times before. "I'll never forget that voice. I was losing. It wasn't going my way. I could tell the judge was mad. It was all over. And then, like an angel, I heard this voice from the back of the courtroom" since he is telling the story to me, he varies from the usual version and adds "*your* voice."

"You stood up and told the judge he was wrong. The officer was wrong. That the law was on my side. That I had to win. I thought I was dreaming! Who has the nerve to tell a judge and a cop that they're wrong! I couldn't even understand what you were saying. I was so nervous and all those legal words. But I knew you were helping me. As soon as you sat down everything turned around. I could hardly even hear what the judge was saying my heart was beating so fast, but he said I could go. I was free. I had won."

"I remember." I said slowly. "That was a few years ago."

"You saved me. I'll never forget that voice. And when I heard you talking here, right away I knew. 'That's my angel!' I told myself, 'my angel from court.'"

"Oh. You're so nice! I can't believe you still remember my voice." I'm uncomfortable with the compliments. "It really wasn't such a big deal. It was my job. Well, my job for my clients. I mean, I was in the courtroom anyway, so…" It wasn't my job. I didn't have to say anything. He's right. I didn't have any reason to help him but I did it anyway. "Well, I'm just glad I was able to help."

Very formally he took my hand and shook it, a very serious look on his face. "I can finally thank you for what you did." He looked like he would have gotten down on one knee and kissed my hand if it would have been acceptable.

My mother proudly chimes in, "And it's her birthday today. She's my daughter!"

He looks at my mother, still holding my hand "Your daughter is a good person. She saved me that day." My mother smiles.

I carried the fudge layer cake to the check out clerk, paid, and we got in the car. My mother couldn't stop talking about what just happened. I filled in the details that were coming back to me. I couldn't believe he recognized me by my voice. I can believe he remembered that a lawyer stood up and told a judge he was about to make a mistake. That's memorable. But years later to recognize my voice? I was stunned. An hour after it had happened I probably forgot all about it, but for Mr. Lucero this was an important event in his life. I thought about Mr. Lucero that whole night.

I fell asleep feeling his happiness at finding me. I was experiencing his sense of completion even though I hadn't been aware there was a loose end.

I was hoping that Eli Acosta's story would have a happy ending too.

That years from now he would come up to me in the grocery store and tell me how his life had been going down the drain because of drugs and I shut off the water. Closed the drain. Threw in a life preserver. That thanks to me, he's all better. That's what I was hoping for anyway.

About a month after sending him to jail his paperwork comes across my desk. The Order of Release for me to sign. His aunt has posted his bond and he was getting out. How could this be? I wanted him to stay in jail until his next hearing. He would overdose on the outside. Get an infection that would kill him this time. Go from one high to the next without eating for days. I know he didn't want to be in jail. That he thought I was killing him by putting him there. If his emotions had turned into anger instead of tears when I told him I was sending him to jail, he would have hit me. Kill me for killing him. And now, his aunt had come up with the bond money. Ten thousand dollars maybe. I couldn't remember exactly what I ordered. That would mean one thousand dollars to a bondsman.

I'm holding the unsigned Order of Release out in front of me as I walk to my secretary's desk. "I can't let him out. How did this happen? How could they come up with the money? How could he have a dime? This is terrible! What am I going to do!"

My secretary, bailiff, and court monitor look unimpressed at my rampage. "I'm not going to sign it" I declare defiantly. They know I would never refuse to let him out when the law says I have to.

They have ribbed me ever since I met with Eli privately. They told me I was a sucker. I believed all his garbage about wanting to get better and I felt sorry for him. Just-another-addict-saying-whatever-he-can-to-get-what-he-wants is what they told me. I should know better by now. "He's not my boyfriend" I protested, and it stuck. Now they always refer to him as that.

But I still sent him to jail—I would point out. I *didn't* give him what he wanted—and he wasn't lying—you didn't see his arms, he really was sick. And he was different from the rest of them. He admitted to me that he was an addict. That takes a lot. Sometimes they never do, just keep coming up with excuses and lies about how they're not really using or if they are, it's because of a back problem, or a fake disease, or terrible headaches, or whatever they can come up with. He started with the lies, the tooth ache, but by the end he was admitting that wasn't it, that he was using heroin. That's a big step towards recovery. Some people die without getting to that point of honesty. And so what if I think he can be helped? So what if I *do* like him. Maybe he is the one I can help.

I signed the Release Order. In less than a minute it had the official court stamp on it and was being faxed to the jail. His next court appearance was five weeks away. I didn't think he would make it.

The weeks went by. Lots of addicts among the other criminals paraded in front of me. There were the obvious addict crimes of possession of a controlled substance, distribution of a controlled substance, and possession of drug paraphernalia. The less obviously drug related crimes of burglary, larceny, robbery, shoplifting, and possession of stolen property. Getting things to turn into money to buy drugs. And the even less obvious, assault and battery and unlawful taking of a motor vehicle. These come when you hit your mother/grandmother/father/neighbor when he/she won't give you twenty bucks for drugs and then you take it anyway and take his/her car to go to the dealer's house. That usually only happens when you are in withdrawal.

I had a client who grabbed a pie off the kitchen counter and threw it in his mother's face when she refused to give him the money he demanded, and then, when she slipped on the mess and was struggling to get up he pulled out the tube to her colostomy bag. Things no one would ever do it they weren't needing a fix. Things that later make their mother/grandmother/father/neighbor tell me at sentencing that their loved one is really a good person, he's just bad when he's drunk or on drugs.

I tell them I believe them, and I do believe them, but my problem is figuring out how to keep every one around him safe until he can control his drinking or drugging. Which, for some people, may be never. My solution, jail, often isn't very popular, drawing moans and vicious looks from the audience, sometimes including the victims. This is why judges have secured parking.

I was nearly home after a long day of hearings and my last stop was Wal-Mart.

Ever since becoming a judge shopping wasn't as relaxing as it used to be. When I was just a lawyer it was a time to day dream, focus on the scent of the brown-sugar body scrub, gaze at the different colored bottles of nail polish, or try to figure out which tea would taste better; lemon zest or cinnamon apple.

I would be disturbed only by former clients, law and midwife: the new custody plan is working out great, she's really doing better in school since we made the change; I'm doing so good on probation they're going to end it early; he's been nursing so well now I'm having a hard time weaning him—the opposite of what I told you that night when I called in tears!

People were generally happy to see me. My entire job as a lawyer was about helping my clients get what they wanted. If I did everything right one hundred percent of the people who left my office would be happy.

As a judge I'm lucky if half the people who leave the courtroom are happy. Or not totally angry. Only one side can win, so at least fifty percent of the people who leave my courtroom are unhappy. And even the winners are angry some of the time too. They didn't win as much as they felt they deserved to. I just do what the law tells me, but it's my mouth the words come out of, my signature on the paper, so I get blamed. Now when I go to the store or a restaurant I look around nervously to see if there is anyone I recognize.

There's that woman from the restraining order the other day. Was she the one trying to get the restraining order or was someone getting it against her? Did I grant it? Did I give a lecture about growing up and solving your own problems? Should I ignore her or smile? That man two tables away is looking at me. Now he's whispering to the woman he's with and she's looking at me. I must have had him in court, but for what? Is he mad? Do I need to let him leave first so he doesn't see my car? Some judges have given up on going out. The grocery store at odd hours, and that's it. Lots of times I don't even recognize the people who have been in my court.

When someone sees me and walks the other way, I figure they must have been on the losing end of a case.

When Eli called my name and came up to me in Wal-Mart I was caught off guard. I didn't recognize him. I was walking out of the store, my cart loaded with bags, and he was walking in, a single bag in his hand.

"Judge Raphaelson." I was nearly out the door when I heard it and stopped. I looked back over my shoulder. He was walking towards me, a neutral look on his face. I was frozen not knowing if I should run, grab my cell phone and call 911, or wait for him to take three more steps and be next to me.

A smile started to grow on his face. I'll wait.

"Judge, is that you? I'm so glad to see you!" He's putting out his hand for me to shake. I'm starting to recognize him. His face is fuller. He's cleaned up. He's wearing a new pair of jeans and a clean red sweat shirt. It's the guy with the arms. The crying, the fake tooth ache, the heroin, the parents. They guy I didn't want to let out. He's alive. He's happy. He's no longer the skeleton who has only drugs for breakfast, lunch and dinner. Now I'm smiling.

"How are you?" I say as I shake his hand.

"I'm good. Really good." He opens the bag he's holding to show me a folded pair of new blue jeans. "I'm returning these, they're not the right size. See I got a job and I'm making a little money. I'm working at a lumber yard. I'm trying to get some new clothes and make myself better little by little." He pulls at the front of his sweat shirt, "this is new too. It's not much, but I'm trying." This is exactly what I had hoped for. I want to go back into the store and buy him new shoes.

"Well, that's wonderful. I have to say I was worried when I saw you were getting out. I didn't know what to expect."

"I'm clean. You can piss test me right now." He has a big smile on his face. "I've been waiting to be tested. I've been staying clean to show you."

"I don't need to test you. I can tell you're clean. You look a lot better." He looks down, a mixture of embarrassment and pride. "You know you have court next week. Thursday morning." I say, like a mother.

Even though he's not acting like a threat, I still want to keep our conversation professional. The shorter the better. I'm still his judge and his case isn't over. I push my purse strap back up on my shoulder to show I'm ready to leave. I want this to end on a good note. I don't want him to remember how mad he was when I told him I was putting him in jail. How he said it would kill him. That I was killing him. "Well" I say slowly, to lead up to 'I have to get going now' when he interrupts me.

"One more thing." His smile has disappeared and his tone is more serious. He wraps his hand around the handle of my cart so I won't try to move it. He's not touching me, but close to it. He starts talking again, softer than before, "I want to thank you."

I hesitate, wondering. The last contact we had was him begging me not to put him in jail and me doing it anyway. "Thank me for what?"

A long pause and he looks directly into my eyes, "Thank you for saving my life."

I'm stunned. I can tell he's still talking but I can't really hear everything he's saying. Transferred to a bigger jail. In the infirmary for two weeks. Medical detox. Got everything out of me. Felt like shit, but then better. Like myself. Ate two trays at every meal. Got my energy back. Like a new me. No, like the old me. Aunt couldn't believe it. Hard to get a job. Don't care what I do. Honest money. Proud of who I am again. Never would have done it on my own. Thank you. Scared. Angry. Jail. You. Me. Listened. Cried. Angel.

You.

Angel.

Saved my life.

I'm stammering "No, you. *You* did it. *You* decided to change. I didn't do anything. It was you... I, I -"

He smiles again and purposely interrupts my minimizing "I'm glad I ran into you. Thank you." He nods politely and walks into the store. I absentmindedly push my cart out the door, find my car, and load the bags in the back seat. I sit in the driver's seat a long time before starting the car. It's not until a few hours later when I'm lying in bed with a book open, but not really reading, that I let myself believe that maybe he was right. Maybe I did save his life. Maybe it was me. At least a little.

Maybe helping Eli is the whole point of this job. The reason I set my self up for the criticisms of lawyers, former friends, complaining with equal disgust that I am both too easy on criminals and too hard. My sentences are too light or too harsh depending on whether you are overhearing the prosecutors or the defense attorneys.

Maybe helping Eli is the reason I allow myself to be the target of complaining letters to the newspaper. I can pretend they don't affect me, that I know they're just sour grapes from losing in court, but still, the hateful words in the letters swirl around as part of the slow tornado of worries that crowd my head and my heart every night.

Maybe helping Eli is the reason I've put myself in the position of getting a phone call from the Sheriff's Department saying they would be doing drive by welfare checks at my house all night in response to what they called a "credible" threat against one of the other judges in the district. Why I overhear my staff debating the best time to show me the threatening letter that came in today's mail (I hope you get killed by a drunk driver you arrogant bitch). Why I even consider carrying a gun.

If the reason I risk angering all of those people in court is to help this one person get off of heroin, then it's worth it. If the reason I put myself and my family in danger every day is so Eli can feel the pride of wearing clothes he bought with his own money, then it's worth it. And if all of the tired nights I'm woken up by the police coming to my door with a search warrant to be signed is so Eli can feel like someone will notice whether he lives or dies, then it's worth it.

I want the story to end here. Eli didn't want to go to jail. I sent him there anyway. For his own good. And my maternalistic 'I know better than you' attitude actually worked! He realized that he had hit the bottom, gotten off of drugs with the help of the jail medical staff, and he's on his way back up. And I had something to do with it. I can make a difference in this job. This is the point of all of it. *This* is why I wanted to be a judge; to change lives for the better. A happy ending for both of us if only it would end right now.

Next Thursday comes and I call his case. State of New Mexico versus Eli Acosta, D-117-CR-4749-371R. The prosecutor stands and announces her name. Eli's attorney stands, says his name, and then looks behind him to the audience.

"I haven't seen him yet this morning judge. Umm." This is the point where I should issue a Bench Warrant for his arrest. The lawyer is trying to make excuses for Eli's absence to prevent this. "Well, when he was here before judge he was taken into custody. He would have been told his next court appearance was at one o'clock in the afternoon, with the other defendants in custody. He wouldn't know to come in the morning with the out of custody defendants. Umm."

"Have you had any contact with him since he's been out? Did you tell him the new time?" I ask, hoping the answer is no. An excuse for me not to issue the warrant.

"I haven't had any contact with him. I didn't tell him he had to come in the morning."

"Well, I've had contact with him. I ran into him in Wal-Mart recently. Most people turn the other way when they see me, but he came up to me." A chuckle from the audience. "He looked good. I'm sure he just has the date or time wrong. I'm not going to issue a warrant. Let's just reset this and Sir, you or someone else from the public defender office can get in touch with him and let him know when to be here."

I wanted Eli to be at the hearing to proudly describe his turnaround. I wanted him to say his boss has made him full time. That he's bought himself new work boots, another pair of jeans. That he's happy with the little things in life; a delicious fish taco from the mobile restaurant that parks around the corner from his simple apartment. That he doesn't even crave the drugs anymore. He feels like he has his life back. That being in jail, going through the medical detox, looking at the other inmates and being afraid of where he was headed, eating three meals a day and remembering the sweet tired feeling of a too full stomach, that all of that has resulted in personal success. That my taking the time to listen to him and do what I believed deep down would help him, despite his protests to the contrary, made a difference in his life. Made THE difference in his life. I want him to say all of this in front of the packed courtroom. In front of everyone who has ever thought anything bad about me. I want Eli to turn to the newspaper editor, who would only be sitting in the courtroom in my self satisfied make believe version of these events, and tell him that he had left drugs behind and I was a part of it.

Eli didn't show up to his rescheduled hearing. This time I did issue a warrant for his arrest, and eventually the police found him. He was dragged back to court, in an orange jumpsuit and handcuffs. He was thinner again. Not as bad as the first time I saw him, yet, but on his way there. The prosecutor recommended probation since it was his first felony offense. I quietly sentenced him, not able to look directly at him the entire hearing. I was embarrassed for both of us.

Months later at a legal conference in Santa Fe I was one of the local judges speaking on a panel about Drug Court. There were judges from all over the Country. The judges from New York were describing their success. How the addicts just needed someone to notice, an authority figure, like a judge, to say "good job for staying clean. I'm proud of you. I knew you could do it. You're too smart to waste your life on drugs." How most of the people who complete their programs don't re-offend. How the money they spend on counselors is far less than the money they would have spent on a lifetime of incarceration. How as judges the favorite part of their job is Drug Court because of all the happy endings.

It's been a long time since I had a happy ending. What am I doing wrong, I thought. Most people who have completed my Drug Court program have re-offended. I run my program according to the National Guidelines just like every other judge, but in my court the magic formula doesn't seem to work. I just heard about one graduate who is selling drugs out of the drive-up window at the fast food restaurant where he works.

Another one I recently had in court on a probation violation for using heroin and cocaine at a Halloween party. She had been such a success story when she kicked drugs that some local organization bought her a house so she and her teenaged children could have a decent place to live. There was a long newspaper article with pictures. One of the lamps I had given her in the background. Her father came to her Drug Court graduation ceremony. He had completed Drug Court a few months earlier.

Late one night a police officer presented me with an arrest warrant he wanted signed so he could pick up a guy who had gone into a five and dime, put a knife to the clerk's neck, and made her empty the register. I didn't recognize the name, but when I saw the picture, I remembered him from Drug Court.

The one who was on trial for accidentally killing a friend after a drug deal went bad. He was planning to beat him up but lost control. He tried to burn the body to hide the evidence. He was only a kid when I had him in Drug Court a few years earlier. I mistakenly called him by his first name when he was before me for the murder.

It seemed like everyone re-offended. Drug Court was a way to stop using drugs while you were in the program; being drug tested every few days, going to counseling nearly every day, meeting with a probation officer a few times a week, and being in front of the judge every week, risking going to jail right away if you had violated any rules in the past few days. After they graduated from the program, they went right back to the needle. I had convinced myself to redefine "success" as staying clean during the nine months of the program, not necessarily afterwards.

At the conference I told one of the judges from New York that she was describing a dream world. That I didn't have the kind of long term success she was enjoying in her program. That nearly everyone went back to using. That I was starting to dread going to Drug Court every week wondering who I was going to learn was positive on a drug test, or had gotten arrested for dealing. That my initial enthusiasm for the program was almost completely replaced with "'what's-the-point,' I'm just going to end up sending them to prison eventually anyway. Why put it off." The days of me secretly buying winter coats for the cold ones and paying for the cost of the GED test for the others were over.

"It's so depressing" I confided in her "we have a lot of heroin here. Even the teenagers are using it. I have fourteen year olds who are already addicted. They see their older relative doing it and they join in. Sometimes they learn from their parents. The first time a twisted birthday present from Mom or Dad. How most teenagers experiment with beer or marijuana, around here they experiment with heroin."

"Wow. Heroin" she mumbles and tilts her head like she's thinking. "We don't see that very much. Lots of cocaine, but not heroin. That's rare." She shakes her head from side to side "I think you need in-patient treatment for that. Really get the person away from the situation." She pauses and thinks some more. "That must be hard to see. Teenagers on heroin? That's extreme. I don't know about Drug Court for *that*." She's thinking out loud. "Yeah, in-patient treatment. Definitely in-patient. You would have to get them out of the environment completely. Even then, that's a hard one to solve."

I should have felt a weight lifted. We have worse drugs than in New York! No wonder I see so many failures. It's not me, not the program, not some inadequacy in the way I'm crafting sentences, it's the strength of the particular drug. Heroin is just too strong for standard treatment to overcome. But instead of feeling like I'm off the hook I feel even more depressed.

As a judge I have power. I'm smart. Everything I do is part of my brilliant plan to help. I have control over hundreds of people's lives. I order them to do this and not that. With the quick, squiggly line that's my signature I can put someone in jail for disobeying me. I should be able to change people for the better. I should be able to make Eli keep that poison needle out of his moldy arm. I want to save Eli like I saved Mr. Lucero that day. I want to be his voice to never forget. I want to be Eli's angel too. But I can't. Maybe no one can. Maybe not even Eli.

I haven't had him in court yet for his probation violation. I can keep him in jail, send him to treatment, or put him back on probation.

It's his life. I think I'll let him choose. Perhaps he already has.

2

The Baby in the Pink Blanket

"Let her hold her baby until it dies." This came out a little louder than I had planned, and somewhat firmer as well. It was the third time I had asked that her new baby be brought to her and I was getting impatient. I couldn't leave the mother's bedside until I delivered the placenta, so I was calling to the Ugandan midwife across the room instead of getting the baby myself.

It was my fourth day volunteering as a midwife in the maternity ward of this large hospital in Uganda. New babies are taken across the delivery room to be weighed on the antiquated scale. The midwife then wraps the baby in the blanket the mother has brought with her and lays the new bundle on the counter next to the scale. The baby will stay there for about ten minutes until a relative shyly walks past the three side-by-side beds in the communal delivery room and politely asks the midwife if she can take the baby to the post partum ward to wait for the mother. If it is an older woman she will respectfully kneel on the floor, looking up as she speaks to the midwife. If I am the only midwife in the room, no one will bother asking. Everyone rightly assumes that I don't speak the local language. In the unlikely situation that the mother has come to the hospital alone, the baby will stay on the counter until the mother delivers her placenta, gets a shot in her thigh with anti-hemorrhage medication (that she has herself purchased and brought with her to the hospital in case the hospital is out, which is usually the case), and then gets herself cleaned up and dressed. Within about fifteen minutes of the delivery she will be walking slowly down the hall to the large post partum ward, a midwife or nurse next to her carrying the baby.

It was this mother's first baby. It was big, and it was in the unusual position of being face up. All of this conspired to make it that much more difficult to get out. Someone had called for the doctor, maybe an hour ago, because it was taking so long for the baby to come. We wanted her to be evaluated for a cesarean. Also, the amniotic fluid that had been leaking out of her was mixed with thick meconium; the little pieces of intestinal garbage that had been collecting inside of the baby prenatally. Instead of being clear, the fluid was dark green and had little green and brown lumps in it. A lack of oxygen to the baby had caused it to come out before the birth. Now it was part of the fluid. Not only was this a sign that the baby was likely going to be born in some sort of distress, but it was also imperative that the pieces of meconium be removed from the baby's throat before it takes the first breath and the pieces get sucked into its lungs.

I knew from my previous days working in the maternity ward that there was only one doctor in town who could perform a cesarean. He did it the old fashioned way, with a large vertical incision, but it worked. Since I had been at the hospital he had been called on a few times before and I had seen it take an hour or more for him to come. Just yesterday I had delivered mal-positioned twins while we waited for the doctor to arrive. I had acted more out of necessity than choice when a tiny arm popped out of the mother as we waited. With some difficulty I repositioned the baby, delivered it, and then its breech sibling a few minutes later. Although I had enjoyed the challenge of the delivery, I had hoped that this type of delay wouldn't happen again, when the results might not be so good.

Here it was the day after the twins and I was again going to be doing a delivery with complications before the doctor arrived. I stood next to the mother and smiled. The local midwife looked through the mother's bag under the bed. Fortunately the mother had brought with her two pairs of sterile gloves, as instructed. The hospital was routinely out. We each put on a pair. I would not take these gloves off until I had delivered the baby, tied and cut the cord, delivered and disposed of the placenta, dried and weighed the baby, cleaned up the blood and fluids on the delivery bed and floor around it, helped the mother wipe herself clean, and rinsed the blood out of the little metal pan I had used to carry the placenta. If I took off my bloody gloves in the middle of any of this there would not be a replacement pair. On my first day I had delivered a baby using only one hand when I was able to find only one glove in time for the birth. In the United States I probably change my gloves about twenty times during a labor and delivery. I have never counted because it has never mattered.

Although we had been telling this woman not to push any more than she absolutely had to, hoping the baby could wait for the doctor, her contractions were pushing the baby and the head was starting to poke out. Gloves on, I said *sindica*, the Lugandan word for 'push.' The delivery was obviously imminent so there was no longer any point in trying to delay it. The mother pushed hard but it wasn't enough. The mother wasn't making a sound. This was just another hard part of life and complaining wouldn't make it any easier. With difficulty I pushed her skin back over the large head while her efforts pushed the head forward. Finally the whole head was out.

More meconium came leaking out around it. For the few hours I had been seeing the meconium I had wondered if the baby would be born dead or alive. There was no equipment to monitor the heart during labor, so I could only wait and see. The large body didn't come out spontaneously. Between the mother pushing and me twisting and pulling, we got the baby out and I put it on the bed between her legs.

The other midwife was beside me, at the mother's shoulder, and there were four nursing students crowded at the end of the bed, leaning on the white paint chipped metal rail. I could see the baby wasn't breathing and I put my fingers lightly across the chest to feel. A slow heart beat. If the baby didn't start breathing the heart would slow down and eventually stop. The first step to getting the baby to breathe was stimulation through touch; rubbing my hand up and down its spine.

But before I got the baby to breathe I needed to clear the meconium out of its throat so it wouldn't get sucked into the lungs and plug up the air openings. Meconium Aspiration Syndrome. It was deadly.

A long suction tube that goes deep into the throat is ideal. Nothing like this was available. The best I could do was use a bulb syringe. It would only reach to the back of the throat, not down it, but maybe somehow it would be enough. I grabbed the faded orange bulb syringe, squeezed the air out and put it as deep into the back of the throat as I could. I released the pressure and waited for the bulb to fill up with meconium. I pulled the bulb out of the mouth and squirted it onto the bed next to the baby. Only air came out. I squeezed the air out and again put it deep into the baby's throat. The bulb expanded and I pulled it out and squirted it onto the bed. Again, only air came out. Where was the meconium? Why wasn't it being sucked into the syringe? I tried one more time and still nothing. I dropped the bulb syringe on the bed. It was useless.

I felt the heart and it was still beating. More slowly than before. If this baby didn't start breathing soon the heart would stop. The local midwife tapped my shoulder. She had picked up the discarded bulb syringe and now held it up in front of me. She pulled at it so I could see the large crack that went half way around the bulb. All it could do was suck air in through the crack, not meconium in through the tip. Not only was it the wrong piece of equipment to begin with, but it didn't even work right!

I stared down at the baby. I could feel the heart slowing beneath my fingers. I thought if ever there was a perfect occasion to freeze time and consult the world's leading medical ethicists, this was it.

If I did nothing, the baby would die.

If I stimulated the baby to breathe, the heart rate would normalize and the breathing would become regular, but meconium would get into the lungs, and then the baby would die.

The best choice, the correct answer on any test, the life saving routine that I had practiced repeatedly in certification classes and done many times in real life, is to suction out the meconium from down deep in the throat, and *then* stimulate the baby to breathe. I know what to do. I know why. I know how. And I also know that because of the circumstances, I can't.

I glance up the bed from the baby and see the mother's face. She is flat on her back without even a pillow. She is craning her neck to look at her still baby on the end of the bed. I hope the answer will somehow become clear. And soon. That I will have a vision, or hear a voice, or in some other way know what God, or whomever, wants me to do. I want the powerful spirits in charge of life and death to send me a message. I want to be told what I am *supposed* to do.

The seconds pass by and I get nothing. All I see are the faces of the people around me, watching to see my next move. All I hear is the midwife breathing into my left ear and the huddle of students breathing into my right. There is not going to be a sign. No flash of inspiration. No inner voice. No voice at all except the laboring woman in the next bed, moaning. This is not a spiritual moment. It is just me standing over a dying baby.

Again I put my fingers across the chest and feel the heart beating. It is slower than it should be, but it is still beating. The baby is alive. I decide to try to save it.

I rub the palm of my hand hard up and down the spine. It doesn't take a breath. I flick at the feet with my fingers. Still no breathing. I squeeze the little mouth into a pucker and lean down over it. I can't touch its lips with mine. Too risky for HIV transmission. I blow down into the mouth from a few inches away. This is ridiculously ineffective but I can't think of any other way to get air into this baby. I do this a few times and try rubbing it again. Nothing.

"Can someone get me the stethoscope?"

I had seen there was one stethoscope, and one leaky blood pressure cuff in the entire maternity ward. Both pieces of equipment were brought out and used only in very serious situations, as if they could be used up if not rationed. No one moves from the bed. I am probably talking too quickly for anyone to understand my English.

More slowly I repeat myself "The stethoscope please." I can at least monitor the crisis even if I can't fix it. Still no movement from any of the staff. No real point anyway.

Then the local midwife says something to one of the students in Lugandan and points towards the counter. The student bangs around in the drawers while I am futilely blowing into the baby's open mouth. The heart is slowing, but still beating. The student returns with an ambu bag. I am shocked. A little round mask with a bag attached that I can squeeze to push air into the lungs. This is like a caveman using a microwave oven. It is totally incongruous. Normally I would hook the mask up to an oxygen tank, but of course there isn't one. Even pushing room air into the lungs is a big improvement. Where did this come from?

The mask is a little too big for the baby but I squish it around the mouth and nose to try to seal up the gaps. I squeeze and I hear much of the air leak out around the mouth. I move my fingers some more to try to make a tight seal with the mask. I squeeze and I see the chest rise slightly. I keep bagging and then stop to see if the baby is breathing on its own. Nothing, but the heart is faster. I put the mask back over the face and squeeze. No chest rise. Nothing getting in the lungs. I move the baby's head to make sure it is in a perfectly straight line with the neck and tilted back just a bit, opening the airway fully. I squeeze again. The chest rises a little but I hear air leaking out of the sides of the mask. I rearrange my fingers again to seal up the gaps. I squeeze the bag and both sides of the chest rise. I don't hear any air leaking out. I keep bagging until I hear the baby make a little gurgle. I move the mask and start rubbing the baby's back again and talking to it.

"Come on little one, you can do it. Time to start breathing."

As long as I rub he keeps taking breaths in response to the discomfort. When I stop, so does his breathing. After about a minute he is breathing on his own. I feel the heart and the rate is normal. The midwife and the students are smiling. I can tell they don't know how I did that.

I continue to stare down at the baby's chest and am relieved to see that it keeps rising and falling. For an instant I forget about the meconium I pushed into the lungs and am flush with happiness at the results of the improvised resuscitation. But my satisfaction doesn't last long.

Within a minute of breathing on his own he makes the first hard gasp, sucking so hard I can hear it but not getting any air into his lungs. Then five or six slow, evenly spaced, normal breaths. Maybe I didn't just see that. Maybe it was just my fear. But then there is another. This unmistakable hard gasp interrupting the peaceful breathing sequence. The other midwife and the nursing students are still smiling. I am not. One gasp can be an accident. Two is a pattern.

I shake my head slowly from side to side. My shoulders droop as I look at the baby and wonder what I have done by saving him. Saving him just so he could die.

"Agonal respirations" I say softly, assuming that I am only putting words to what everyone else is thinking. I look up at the students. They are almost jovial while they touch the new baby and talk about him in Lugandan. They obviously don't understand the significance of what they are seeing.

"Those are agonal respirations"—I imitate the hard gasp in case they haven't learned the term yet—"they are a sign of impending death" I announce quietly in something that is supposed to be a teaching voice.

Someone carries the baby off behind me to the scale. The normal post delivery routine. I am staring at the empty spot on the bed. The ventilating bag is still there. Some do-gooder foreigner must have donated it. Someone like me who mistakenly assumed the midwives would know what to do with it. I'm sure this is the first time it has been used.

I look back towards the scale to see the baby. It has been wrapped in a fluffy pink blanket that one of the nursing students dug out of the mother's bag. The pink bundle is on the counter next to the scale. The delivery over, the students have left the room and it is now just me and the local midwife. I am waiting next to the mother to deliver her placenta.

Usually there would be just one midwife doing all of the deliveries that day, but since I am here volunteering this week, we are both doing deliveries. I am calling to the local midwife to bring the baby to the mother. Being educated, she speaks English. Sort of. She is sitting at a wobbly table in front of the long counter writing the statistics on the delivery into a large book that will be the permanent record. She is sitting on a wooden bench with metal legs, only the wooden part that is the actual bench is missing so she balances herself on the two bars of metal, one running between the back legs and one between the front. The wooden bench used to be screwed across the top of the bars. To her left is a sink with only cold running water. Today there is a small end of a bar or soap next to it. Yesterday there wasn't.

The blue Formica counter with the scale and the baby is surprisingly devoid of medical equipment. It's not that the equipment is hidden, it's just that there isn't much. The mothers are instructed that when they are in labor they are to bring with them to the hospital everything that will be needed for the delivery; two pairs of sterile gloves for the midwife to wear, a new disposable razor blade for cutting the cord, a piece of cloth for drying the baby, a blanket for wrapping the baby, a cloth to be used as a sanitary pad after the delivery, and most precious of all, a large square piece of plastic that the mother will lie on when she delivers.

It looks like a plastic trash bag with the sides slit open. When unfolded it nearly covers the cracked vinyl wrapped mattress but for a few inches at the top and bottom. I had already seen laboring women coarsely scolded for omitting this from their bag of supplies. The best I can tell, the point of the piece of plastic is to minimize the mess from the birth. No one has explained any of the routines to me. The local midwives assume that all hospitals function like this. They were awed when I told them that in the United States the hospital supplies all the drinking water and juice the mother wants. I didn't have the heart to tell them about the hot meals. Here there are no sheets or absorbable pads to put on the bed under the mother, so the blood or amniotic fluid that leaks out of the mom gets caught on the plastic. By the time the delivery is over the mother is lying in a puddle, her bottom and back completely soaked.

I have figured out that I am supposed to fold the edges of the plastic in towards the mother once it gets wet. The idea is to trap the liquids from spilling over the edge of the bed onto the floor. This is an art I haven't mastered. After every delivery I find myself cleaning the floor next to the bed with an old cloth soaked with the bleach from the small bottle the mother has also been forewarned to bring.

In response to my request that she bring the dying baby to its mother, the local midwife barely looks up from the birth ledger book and asks politely in her slightly off English, "What is this?"

I spoke more slowly this time, but with the same insistent tone as before. The baby was breathing now but I knew it wasn't going to last. If he was only going to live a few minutes he should spend that time in his mother's arms. All of my anger, guilt, and uncertainty about having just pushed deadly meconium into the baby's lungs was disguised as the frustration of not being able to get the mother and baby together.

I don't know how long it will take for this baby to die; a few minutes, a few hours. I can't imagine it could be as long as a whole day. I have no personal experience with this kind of death. This situation would never be allowed to progress so far in the United States. Even with the home deliveries I do I bring a disposable tube specially designed for removing meconium from the throat. I put one end deep down the throat and suck on the other end. There is a one way valve that prevents anything I suck out from reaching my mouth. There is a plastic cup attached in the middle of the tube that catches the fluid. Each tube is sterile and sealed in a plastic pouch. It costs about a dollar. I have a drawer full of them.

I was genuinely upset that the baby and mother were in the same room, but weren't together, but that was just part of it:

I was upset that I had pushed that meconium into the baby's lungs when I knew what it would do to him.

I was upset that I didn't have the equipment to do the resuscitation the right way.

I was upset that the local midwife didn't seem to know what I was doing when I was resuscitating the baby.

I was upset that the local midwife didn't seem to believe me when I kept insisting that the baby was going to die.

I was upset that the mother and I didn't have a common language so that I could tell her the baby was going to die.

I was upset that the baby was, in fact, going to die.

I was upset that the mother had a big laceration from how I had to do the delivery, but there wasn't even one package of sutures for me to stitch her with.

I was upset that the doctor had been called an hour earlier to do the delivery and hadn't arrived until after it was over, and then left immediately after peeking his head in the door and seeing the baby was out.

I was upset that the whole hospital smelled like urine.

I was upset that I had bathed that morning by standing over a drain in the bathroom floor and splashing cold water on me that came from a spigot sticking out a few feet up the wall.

I was upset that to the locals this level of indoor plumbing would be a luxury.

I was upset that at home, in my three bathrooms, the toilets are filled with water clean enough to drink.

I was upset that this baby was dying solely because of poverty. I was upset that anybody should be that poor.

And for all kinds of other reasons that I couldn't figure out at that moment, I was upset. It all got funneled into the mother not being able to hold her baby.

"Let her hold her baby. It's going to die. She should hold her baby before it dies."

The local midwife just smiles at me, amused with what she must have thought was my overreaction. "She will see him later" and she looks down again and continues writing in the book. Along with the injustice of the baby dying for lack of a suction tube, it is doubly unjust that I have to try so hard to convince everyone that he is dying.

As I tugged on the cord coming from between the mother's legs and instructed her one last time to push, *sindica*, I brought her placenta out of her and placed it in the small metal bowl on the end of the bed. I carried the bowl across the room, past the midwife, and past the baby, to the metal bucket where the other placentas had been disposed of. I slid this one onto the pile, holding the lid of the bucket at an angle hoping to prevent any blood from splashing back at me. At the end of the previous day I had seen the cleaning lady disappear with the bucket. I don't know what happened next, but eventually the bucket reappeared, empty.

I walked past the baby to the sink where I deposited the bloody metal tray. I would rinse it out later. Swish a little bleach in it, if there was some available. I took off my gloves. Rinsed my hands in the cold water. Warm air streamed into the room from the bank of open windows over the counter. Ancient tan and green linen curtains were blowing over the counter from the wind. I had seen others dry their hands on the curtain above the sink, but I shook mine for few seconds and then wiped them on the front of my scrubs. I went back to the baby. I pulled the blanket back from his chest. His color was good, but he was still gasping intermittently.

"Is there any way to give him oxygen?" I had asked the other midwife.

"In Theatre there is oxygen." The operating room. It was in another building. I hadn't been there but I had walked past the sign.

"Can we bring the baby there?"

She shrugged her shoulders like something like that just wasn't done.

"I'll sit with him if no one else can go. I'll stay the whole time and give him the oxygen" I offered hopefully.

She said maybe, but I knew it wouldn't happen. Even if it did, they probably only had a few hours worth of bottled oxygen, at most, and would rightly want to save it for surgeries.

I walked back to the mother to help clean her up.

"Thank you" she said, tentative about her English.

By accident, in acknowledging her, my sadness resulted in me making more of a frown than a smile. Then, as I was folding in the edges of her plastic sheet, trying to drain all the liquids around her body to a section in the middle, she said something else.

"Why-baby-no-cry?"

This question must have been the result of a tremendous effort of all of her English skills. I thought how I could answer using simple words that she might understand.

"The baby is sick. The lungs-" and I point to my chest and take an exaggerated breath so that my lungs visibly inflate and deflate "—the lungs are broken." I can't tell if she understands.

"The baby will die." I say slowly. Her expression doesn't change.

"Dead." I say. Still no change.

I try again, hoping she will understand. "Not alive." I figure I will know if I am successful in this attempt at communication if the mother starts to cry.

Another midwife who had walked in during the resuscitation was looking in a cupboard for something. She knew the basic situation. I called to her and asked if she would translate.

"Tell her the baby will die. She doesn't understand me. Tell her because of the meconium in the lungs, the baby is sick."

The midwife says something quickly in Lugandan. It takes only a few seconds. The mother nods her head. I am uncertain that the midwife actually told her.

"You told her the baby will die? You told her about the meconium?"

"Yes." and she walks out.

The first midwife is still writing in the record book so I go get the baby myself and bring him back to the mother. I put him in her arms. She looks at him and again tells me thank you. She can't possibly understand.

After placing the baby in the mother's arms, I took it back from her only a few minutes later so she could climb down from the high bed, wrap herself in a clean length of cloth from her bag, and waddle down the hall to the post partum ward.

She looks for an empty bed among the thirty or so in the room. Having picked one out in the back, she covers it with the sheet she brought from home, and lies down with her baby. Her family has followed her and they roll out thatch mats on the floor around the bed, and unpack the food and water they have brought. They will all spend the rest of the day and the night here; the woman on the bed with the baby, the family on the floor taking care of them both with whatever they have packed in their bags.

It had been a few hours since the delivery and I had been in the delivery room the whole time. No one was delivering so I walked through the post partum room, past rows of beds and the corresponding families spread out on the floor around them, all the way to the back of the room where the mother had claimed a bed. As I walk through the ward heads turn to watch me. Little children smile and excitedly say *Muzunga*, white person. I came up next to the bed with the new mother and baby, still wrapped in the fluffy pink blanket, and said hello. The bed was surrounded with people. It looked like a few older sisters, her mother, father, and grandmother. There was a young boy, probably the son of one of the sisters. They all lit up when they saw me.

They couldn't speak any more English than *Hello* and *Welcome*, but I'm sure they had all heard from the mother that I had brought the dead baby back to life. The mother cradled the baby next to her on the bed. He was alive. Through pantomime I told the mother that she should try to feed the baby. Offer him her breast. She and her sisters shook their heads in agreement.

I walked back to the maternity ward not believing that the baby was still alive. Maybe I was wrong and he wouldn't die. Maybe he was one of the few statistically who would not get sick. But surely he would. Those who live do so because they get aggressive intensive follow up treatment in an ICU. This baby couldn't even get a little extra oxygen. But he was alive and he was breathing normally, except for the occasional gasp. Maybe it just didn't affect him the way I thought it would. After all I didn't have any experience with a baby who has aspirated meconium. How would I? I was just going by what I was taught, what it said in books.

A few more hours and my shift would be over. I left for the day without visiting the baby again. I replayed the resuscitation over and over in my head as I lay on my bed, under the tent of white mosquito netting, in the small, simple room that had been rented for my stay. The whirring of the loud ceiling fan combined with the constant drip of the water in the toilet tank in the tiny bathroom just a few steps from the end of the bed, eventually lulled me to sleep.

My first thought in the morning was of the baby. The dead baby. I didn't want to get out of bed. I didn't want to go back to the hospital. I was just a volunteer. I didn't have to go back. But I didn't even know how to contact the driver who would be coming to the hotel in an hour to pick me up. He didn't speak English. My second day, on the drive to the hospital, I tried to tell him to pick me up an hour earlier than he had the previous day. He kept smiling and saying 'Jenny Guest House,' the name of the hotel. I got picked up at the regular time.

I washed with the cold water, ate four bananas and a passion fruit, took my malaria pill, put a little bottle of hand sanitizer in my pocket and waited for the driver.

When I arrived back at the hospital I headed straight to the maternity ward. I didn't see any point in going into the post partum ward. The baby most likely died in the night and the mother and her family would have gone home, maybe taking the baby with them, or leaving it for the hospital to dispose of. I didn't know the procedure.

One of the student nurses who had been at the birth the previous day was in the maternity ward. She smiled when she saw me and immediately asked, "have you seen your baby?" I shook my head with confusion.

"The baby yesterday" she clarifies. "The one you save. *Your* baby."

"It's still alive?"

"Yes. They are in the ward."

I was wrong. That baby wasn't going to die after all. Now I'm glad no one seemed to understand me when I insisted that the baby was dying, was having agonal respirations. Thanks to the language barrier, instead of being the idiot who thinks a healthy baby is a dying baby, I'm just the hero who saved the baby. Yeah. I'm great! There aren't any laboring women in the maternity ward so I turn around and walk back down the hall to the post partum ward.

Sure enough, way in the back, I see the mother and her family still gathered around the last bed, the bright pink blanket jumps out at me in the otherwise dull room. Someone in the family sees me walking their way and the others all turn around, smiling. No doubt they are happy to see the foreign midwife who saved their baby.

The family is sitting in a circle on mats on the floor next to the bed. They are eating what looks like cooked potatoes from chipped white bowls. The mother is in the circle. She is kneeling. Good, she is keeping her legs together. That will help the tear heal. The baby is on the bed, a female relative sitting next to him. I am smiling and I pull back the blanket to look at his face. He is alive. His color is good, no hint of blue that would show he wasn't getting enough oxygen. He's calm and sleeping. Not struggling to take a breath or even gasping—at least during the short time I was looking. He is not going to die! I was so wrong and I couldn't be happier.

Now I remembered the little round growth next to his pinkie. The accidental start of a sixth finger. It stuck out of his hand like the tip of an eraser. I had noticed it at the delivery. It is genetic and is no comment on the baby's health. Normally I would have tied a string tightly around the base of the bump to cut off the blood flow. That would make it painlessly fall off and his hand would look completely normal with only a small dot of shiny skin where the growth had been. I didn't bother to tie it off yesterday because I didn't think the baby was going to live. Why worry about him getting teased when he's twelve if he's never going to be twelve.

I pull the little hand out of the blanket and point out the growth to the woman on the bed. I hold up my finger to indicate that I will be right back. She shakes her head in acknowledgement and smiles. I walk back to the delivery room to find some string.

I ask the midwife for the thin strong thread used for stitches and tell her what it's for. She opens and closes a series of near empty drawers. Then she leaves for a few minutes and comes back empty handed. She says there is none today. She suggests using the little strips of white string we use to tie off the umbilical cord. We both peer into the dented stainless steel canister that houses a pile of these strings.

"It is too big?" she asks me. I know she means too thick.

"I think so. But maybe it will work." We are both mentally tying off the extra finger with this shoelace like material and both realizing that it is probably too thick. "There's nothing else?" I ask, knowing that there isn't and she will confirm I will have to use this.

She shakes her head no. We both shrug our shoulders and I say I will try it. Just then a woman comes in and unfolds her plastic sheet onto the bed closest to the door. She drops her bag on the floor and kicks it slightly so it slides under the bed a few inches. As soon as she gets on the bed she gives a long hard push.

I dive into the bag and push aside blankets and rags and bright pieces of cloth and find two packages of sterile gloves. I open one package and hold it out in front of the midwife. She puts them on. I place the other package on the end of the bed. I will put those on myself once I finish looking in the bag. I come out with a disposable razor blade, wrapped in a flimsy paper package, an injection syringe sealed in its original packaging, and a little brown envelope containing a vial of pitocin. I put all of this on the end of the bed next to a cloth the size of a dishtowel that I will use to dry the baby.

I go to the stainless steel canister and remove two little strips of white string. I put on the second pair or gloves, remove the syringe from the package, break open the glass vial and suck the medicine into the syringe. The other midwife is standing across the bed from me. When the baby is out she places it on the mother's belly. I dry it and turn it on its back so I can get to the cord. I tightly tie one and then another piece of string around the cord about an inch from the baby's belly. I carefully tear away the paper wrapping from the razor blade and slowly slice through the cord. The short stump on the baby bleeds a few drops. The long cord still attached inside the mother bleeds steadily. It won't stop until the spoonfuls still running through the cord are drained out. I put the cord back on the bed where the remaining blood flows into the existing puddle on the plastic between the mother's legs. I read somewhere about a culture that smartly delivers outside on open weave hammocks. All the fluids drain onto the ground.

I carry the baby to the scale along with the torn paper envelope that my sterile gloves were wrapped in, which I have already learned to save. I place the opened paper package on the scale, and put the naked baby on top of that. I slide the weights until I come up with the right kilograms. I wrap the baby in a blanket from the mother's bag and leave it bundled up peacefully on the counter next to the scale.

The midwife has delivered the placenta and is placing it into a small silver bowl she has gone to get from the wet pile next to the sink (oops, I forgot to get that). Once the placenta is in the bowl the midwife walks into the other room to put it in the bucket. I take the syringe with the pitocin, stick it deep into the mother's thigh and push the plunger down, shooting the liquid into the muscle. I should first clean the spot on her leg with alcohol, but there isn't any. The other midwife would ordinarily do all of this herself. I feel lucky that I can spoil her by helping, even if it is only for a few days.

When the plastic sheet has been carefully folded into a wet ball, and the mother has wiped herself off with the cloths from her bag, placed a rag between her legs, and wrapped herself in a colorful length of cloth, draping it expertly around her body and then over her shoulders, I scoop up her baby and we walk together slowly to the post partum ward.

That is when I remember about the growth. And the string. And that I was going to come back in just a minute as I indicated by holding up my one pointed finger. I go back to the delivery room and get a piece of the string. When I am walking towards the family in the back, again they all smile at me. Not only did I save their baby, but I actually came back to fix the finger like I said I would. I cannot disappoint.

I am so happy that he is going to live. That I was wrong. It's a relief that they didn't understand me the day before. The only thing I can imagine that is worse than being told your baby is going to die is being told your baby is going to die when it isn't true. The other midwives weren't ignorant,

I was. They must see babies taking in meconium all the time. They were ignoring my doomsday pronouncements because they knew I was wrong, not because they didn't know about meconium. They were being polite to act like they didn't understand. The alternative would have been to tell me directly I was wrong.

I have the little string in the pocket of my shirt. I pull the pink blanket back from the baby's face. Immediately I see that he is not right. His face is pale and his lips have a hint of blue. He isn't getting enough oxygen. I move the blankets from his chest and look at it move. I see the little chest rising and falling. My instinct is to look at my watch and count the rate, but I don't need to. I can tell he is breathing too fast. Probably twice the normal rate. His skin is sucking in around his ribs as he struggles to breathe. This is the official start of respiratory distress. It will quickly get worse. I was smiling when I approached the bed and I force my mouth to stay in that position. There is now no question that I was right. The baby is not *going* to die, the baby is dying right now.

The family is looking at me. Their warm smiles say the mother told them what happened at the delivery; that the baby came out and it was silent, that the Ugandan midwife didn't do anything, but the *Muzunga* midwife did. Poking and blowing and squeezing a balloon over the baby's face. That for a long time nothing happened, but then eventually, the baby came alive. That the other midwives wouldn't have done anything. That if the *Muzunga* midwife hadn't been there, the baby would be dead. How lucky they were. Not only was I there, but for some reason I decided not to let the baby stay dead.

Should I go find the stethoscope, come back, and listen to the respirations just to confirm what I already know? Should I get one of the nurses to come over and tell the family in Lugandan that the baby is dying? Should I tell the mother to come up off the floor, stop eating and hold the baby, that this would be her last chance? I stay hunched over the baby, holding back the pink blanket from the chest and watching it move too quickly. I remember the little piece of string I had retrieved from my pocket. There's no reason to tie off the extra finger. There's no reason not to.

I pull the little hand out of the pink blanket. I carefully tie the string around the base of the growth. The woman on the bed looks on curiously. I tie it as tightly as I can to be sure to stop all of the blood flow so the procedure will be successful. Maybe performing this needless act that is only for the future will somehow make there be a future.

I look at the proud family and give a nod indicating that I agree they have a beautiful baby. I tuck the hand back into the pink blanket, kiss my fingers and touch them to his forehead, and walk back to the maternity ward. I know that they will leave sometime today and I am hoping it is soon, before he dies. If the last I know of them is that they leave the hospital with a live baby, I can pretend that is how it stays. There is a column in the big statistic book where the midwife indicates the condition of the baby at the time of discharge; either a letter 'A' for alive, or a letter 'D' for dead.

I sit in the delivery room in the spot farthest from the door. I don't want to see the family walk down the hall on their way home. I don't leave to use the bathroom, or to take a short walk around the grounds, past the waiting families camped out on every available piece of ground. I don't leave the limited visual protection that the seclusion of the delivery room provides to me. After a few hours one of the nurses comes in. I have only seen this nurse in the delivery room a few times, looking for supplies. She seems to work mostly in the post partum ward.

She heads straight to the drawers and starts the familiar routine of opening and closing them all looking for something that probably doesn't exist; more gloves, an IV bag, alcohol, bleach, paper towels, a syringe. She reaches into the back of one of the drawers and she takes out the stethoscope. Immediately I know. She needs to listen for a heart beat to confirm that there isn't one.

I did the same thing a few days before after a young woman walked into the delivery room and politely got my attention. She led me to a bed and pointed to the wrapped baby. I had delivered it a few hours earlier. It was premature. When I had put my pinkie finger in its mouth it didn't suck. That reflex hadn't developed yet.

The mother was stretched out on her side, the baby lying in the space between her bent knees and outstretched arm—alongside its former home. I could tell right away it was dead. I felt it and it was cold. I didn't see the chest rise. I went back into the delivery room and found the stethoscope. After listening I looked at the mother and shook my head no. I went back to the book and wrote 'D' in column on her line.

The nurse with the stethoscope had been gone a few minutes. I wanted to follow her to see what bed she went to. But I wanted stay right where I was and disappear. I wanted to pretend I hadn't seen the nurse come in or know what the stethoscope was for. I wanted a mother to walk in pushing so I could focus on something else. I wanted the whole situation to go away. I wanted the string I had tied around the baby's sixth finger to fix its lungs as well. What I did in the end was do nothing.

When the nurse came back a few minutes later with the stethoscope in one hand and the pink blanketed baby cradled in her other, I was still sitting in the corner farthest from the door. She put the lifeless bundle on the counter, the stethoscope back in a drawer, and left. Left me alone with the baby. I didn't have to look any closer to know, but I did anyway.

I had the blanket pulled back from the face and was hunched over the baby, staring, when the nurse returned with two female relatives. I had used up all of my emotion and my head felt empty, my face blank. I backed away from the baby. There was a quick exchange in Lugandan and then one of the women scooped up the baby, put the blanket back over the face, and they left out of the back door, through the room with the bucket of placentas. I had only one more day to work and I didn't want to come back.

Everything else that day went by robotically. The rest of the afternoon at the hospital, the car ride home past the open air markets that lined both sides of the road. Even though the rickety stands piled with fruit, potatoes, used sandals, sheets of cloth, charcoal, fish, chickens (dead and alive), and furniture odds and ends were narrowing the street to nearly one lane, forcing cars to pass by with only inches between them, the ever present motorcycles and bicycles somehow managed to do figure-eights through all of it.

I hardly noticed the plate of rice I ate on the porch of the hotel while writing cryptic notes in the pocket sized memo pad I had brought on the trip as a sort of diary. Under today's date I wrote:

3 vertex deliveries
1 VBAC—classical incision
Resuscitation baby—dead
8,000 shillings for maid to wash three pairs of scrubs, underwear, one bra. No change. Thrilled with the 2,000 shilling tip

I didn't think about the baby. I didn't think about anything. I slept.

The next morning I went into the delivery room and saw the same four nursing students that had been there the previous days. There were no other staff members. The students were chatting in Lugandan when I walked in. They stopped talking and very formally said good morning to me. The one who was sitting on the "good" chair, a wooden school desk chair that amazingly didn't wobble, got up and offered me the seat. No one was quite sure of my position in the pecking order, and there definitely was one as I had seen much fuss over respecting rank. They must have thought I was above them, as the local midwives would be.

I walked past the offered seat and sat on the edge of the table. Maybe a minute later the local midwife came in. The one who had been standing with me at the resuscitation. I had worked with her almost every day. The students again rose, greeted her, and then offered her the same seat they had offered me. She also refused. She was in her street clothes, a beautiful brown and gold cloth wrapped and draped in such a way to make her look like royalty. Her long hair braided tightly with small gold beads woven into the braids that gave the illusion of a flat tiara lying across the top of her head. Her blue scrub dress was hanging on a hook with many other in the store room that was used as a changing room.

We greeted each other. She asked me how late I was working. Four o'clock I told her. That was the time of the afternoon shift change, the time when she would go home and the evening midwife would arrive to take over. She was silent, still standing, and looked to her right at the group of students. The delivery beds were empty.

"My back is hurting" she said slowly. The other day she had mentioned to me that her back had been sore for some time. I told her I had Tylenol at my hotel and I could bring it for her. She said no. Later I figured out that I should have said Panadol, as that is the trade name they are familiar with and Tylenol means nothing to her.

"I should rest in bed" she continued. It was like she was testing everyone's reaction by saying this, talking slowly and looking at our faces. Heads shook up and down sympathetically. Then, what she had carefully been leading up to,

"I am going home into bed."

The students looked shocked. They froze. Taking a day off because your back hurts isn't done. It isn't contagious so you can still work. To spend a work day at home in bed is, well, selfish. Even when the hospital is fully staffed there are barely enough hands to provide the basic care. It would be disrespectful for any of the students to voice an outright objection. Finally one dared to speak.

Her voice was slow and quiet, "Sister" the respectful title that was used for the professional women at the hospital, "who will conduct deliveries?"

The midwife points her finger and throws her arm out to her left, in my direction. She doesn't look at me but keeps her eyes on the group of students. They glance at me, having the same worried thought that I am.

"Sister Senior Midwife. She is in charge. Ask her if you have questions."

Uh-oh. I have some questions.

This was, of course, ridiculous. I could deliver babies as well as the other midwives, but there was a long list of things that I couldn't do that seemed rather crucial to the job of being in charge of the delivery room, the main one being communicating with patients. All I could say was 'push.' I couldn't tell them "get on that bed over there" or "roll on your side" or "you are dehydrated. Is there someone with you who has some water for you to drink?" or "when did you start feeling contractions?" or "is this your first baby?" or "did you bring gloves? I can't find them in your bag" or "I can't read the label on this vial from the pharmacy. I can't inject it unless I know what it is. Go back and tell them you need one with a label that isn't worn off" or a multitude of other phrases that I could imagine being useful.

Another potential problem jumped into my mind. I had pretty much figured out under what circumstances to summon the doctor, mainly if I determined a cesarean was necessary, but I didn't know how to actually do it. The other midwives had called to some phone number and either left a message for him describing the medical situation, and why he was needed, or talked to him directly. Forget that I would be lost trying to work their phone system, I didn't even know his name. I doubt he would even respond to a request by me. I was nobody. It would be professionally irresponsible and unfair to the patients for me to allow this midwife to leave me in charge.

"Go home and rest" I could hear my own voice but didn't know why I was saying this. "I'll take care of everything."

"Thank you Sister." With that, she walked out.

It's done. And when else is she going to be able to take a day off anyway? I can use the students to translate.

Not too much later a laboring woman came in and climbed up on a bed. She pulled up her skirt and began pushing. She wasn't stretched open yet, but I could tell it wouldn't be long until we saw the head. Maybe two or three more pushes. I could tell by looking at her skin that the head was pushing right behind it and making it flat where it used to be puffy. I got on one side of the bed with one of the students, and the other three got on the other. One pulled out two packages of gloves from the mother's bag and handed them to me. I handed one package to the student across from me who was standing beside the mother's bent knee.

"I should examine her?" She asked me.

"If you want to. She's ready. I can tell by looking. See how that skin is" and I pointed to her labia and was going to continue explaining.

"- I should not examine her?"

"Umm. Go ahead. Yes. Examine her and tell me what you find." I was acting as the teacher after all.

The student puts on one of the two gloves from the package. She inserts two fingers into the woman. I rotate my hand so the palm is up and my two fingers are spread far apart, indicating that she should do the same. She moves her fingers like mine. I make a gap between my fingers of ten centimeters.

"This is ten centimeters. Is that the space you feel between the two edges?" I know it is.

"Yes." She takes her fingers out and starts to take off her glove.

"No, no. Leave that on and put on the other." I am putting my gloves on as I say this. The student does as I tell her. Once her second glove is on I take her two hands in mine and place them on the mother.

"This one stays on the bottom, pushing in like this" I put my hand over hers and press in on the skin just below the vagina. "Don't move this hand until the baby is out." I take her other hand and put it above the vagina. "When the head starts to come use this hand to push it down." She starts to move her hands away and I push them back just as I had originally placed them. This time I leave my hands on top of hers pressing with the same pressure she will need to use when the head comes.

The mother pushes and the top of the head starts to come out between the student's hands. She again tries to pull them away and I keep mine firm on top of hers.

"Who is conducting the delivery?" she asks in a panic.

"You are." Her eyes are huge and her mouth drops open as she looks at me across the bed, our faces a foot from each other. She shakes her head no. She has never done this before. I know she is afraid. I remember the feeling. "I'll show you exactly what to do."

More of the head comes out with the next push. She releases some of the pressure on her bottom hand. The skin will tear.

"You have to push hard." I realign her student's hand on the mother's skin and push hard, her hand trapped between mine and the mother. The student's other hand is sort of floating above the top of the head, near where I had put it before. I take it with my free hand, put it firmly on the top of the head, my hand over hers, and push downward.

The other three students are squished along the side of the bed near the mother's head; one next to me and the other two across the bed. They are all leaning in over the mother's belly to see what I am doing with our collective hands.

"The bottom hand pushes in, the top hand pushes down" I remind the student as I continue to exert the correct pressure and directions on top of her hands. The head is out.

I remove my top hand and she takes hers off too and is going to put it to her side. I grab it and slide her index finger down the side of the baby's head to the neck that is still hidden.

"Check for a cord. Do you feel a cord?"

"No."

"Good. Now, after you see the head turn, yes, like that, use this hand" and I grab the top hand again, still pushing her bottom hand in place, "and push down until you see the top shoulder." She is looking at the top of the mother's vagina as are the other students. The baby's neck is out and here comes the round blob that is the top shoulder. "There!" They all nod in agreement.

"Now bring the baby up to mom." I guide her hands to under the baby, and as I have her pulling the baby up towards the mother's stomach, the head just now becoming visible to the mother as she looks between her legs, the rest of the baby slides out. Together we put the baby onto the mother's belly. Just inches above the little baby are the smiling faces of the students, all in a huddle. It starts to cry. The hands of the student who has done the delivery are shaking visibly. I decide someone else should tie and cut the cord.

I am identifying each of the other students with a nod of my head as I assign jobs: you get the towel and dry the baby, you get two pieces of string because you're going to tie the cord, you get the razor blade but tell me when you're ready to cut and I'll show you where and how to keep the blood from spurting.

The student who did the delivery is still standing next to the bed. Her hands aren't shaking as much as before. I decide she is calm enough to deliver the placenta.

"This is how you tell if the placenta is ready to come. Put the side of your hand here on her belly. No, a little lower, exactly where I put mine. Now push down and watch the cord. If it moves back inside, the placenta is still attached. If it doesn't move, it is ready to deliver. This is called the Brandt–Andrews Maneuver." Why did I say that? It doesn't matter what it's called. I'm just showing off. "You don't have to remember that." The student pushes down and the cord moves back inside. Not ready. I have the other students watch as I demonstrate.

The baby needs to be weighed. The three helpers rush off to the scale with the baby. There is a gush of blood from the mother. The placenta has detached and is ready to deliver.

"Did you see that blood? That is from the placenta detaching. Push down again with your hand and look at the cord." It doesn't move. I call the other students over so they can see. I instruct the student who delivered the baby how to deliver the placenta.

Once the placenta is out I have all the students look at the end of the cord. There should be three vessels coming through it. Who knows what they are? Well that's okay, I'll tell you; two arteries and a vein. Look at the size of the placenta, it's big. If you have a big baby, you have a big placenta. If you have a small baby, you have a small placenta.

The students are listening to everything I say and answering the best they can. Sometimes I have to search for a different word when they say they don't understand. They are no longer submissive and formally polite. They have stopped calling me 'Sister Senior Midwife' and call me simply 'Sister.' They are excited. This is much better than learning from a book or watching from across the room.

You, yes you, come over here and let me show you how to give the shot of pitocin. Do you know how it works? The uterus is made of smooth muscle. This drug causes contractions of smooth muscle. Draw two imaginary lines on her thigh like this, then give the shot in the center of the little square you made up here. Put it all the way in, you need to go into the muscle. That's right.

Even after this mother has cleaned up and left, all four of the students walking her and the baby down the hall to the post partum room, the excitement is still in the room. They are now writing in their workbooks the description of the delivery. They have to do this for every delivery they observe, which is the only thing they are supposed to be doing; observing. I write up the paragraph long medical summary in the child's school exam notebook that is used as the mother's chart and they all look over my shoulder as I do it, comparing it to their efforts.

The day continues on with me choosing a different student to do each delivery, my hands over theirs demonstrating the proper movements. During every delivery there is much worried glancing at the door. The students are afraid that if someone walks in and sees them they will get in trouble. I'm sure they are right. I have told them that I am the Senior Midwife so they have to do what I say. They are not terribly comforted by this. We all know that is just building on the initial wrong of the local midwife appointing me the Senior Midwife and going home. I try to reassure them not to worry, that I will say it is all my fault. This is my last day anyway.

It is nearly the end of my shift. The day has passed quickly and I have really enjoyed it. Maybe more than any of the previous days. Helping the students has been like a feeling of life. It has successfully replaced my previous day's feelings of death.

When the next midwife comes at four o'clock for the new shift I stand at the end of each bed with her, reporting the status of each patient. She sits down at the table and assumes control. I smile and wave good bye to the students.

"You come tomorrow?"

"No. This is my last day."

"Thank you. Thank you for the teaching" one student blurts out. The others agree loudly and shake their heads. Then they look over at the other midwife, afraid that they have revealed too much, or that I might say something wrong in response.

I smile at them and say only, you're welcome.

I can imagine the students years from now, hundreds of births later, using the skills I have taught them, maybe remembering back to their first deliveries, with the *Muzunga* midwife literally holding their hands.

3

I Want the Jew Bitch!

"Dear: Sheri A. Raphaelson,
first of all i want to thank you for takeing my case. I
don't know what i would of done if i never called you
thank you very much i greatly appriceate it. God bless!!!"

The letter I eventually got from Davy Rice was like that one,
including the poor spelling and grammar. I usually smile
when I get these and then put them in the file and never
look at them again. The letter from Davy didn't go in his file but in
my desk drawer. I put it near the stack of sympathy cards I bought
in bulk when I saw how many clients or relatives of clients died
early deaths, mostly from drug overdoses, and I was wasting money
and time buying the cards individually. I would pull out Davy's
letter a few times a year when I was feeling particularly hopeless.
Of course it made me feel great to read good things about me, but
that wasn't the purpose of reading the letter. It was to remind me
that there is no such thing as a bad person. To remind me that

there is sometimes a reward for enduring a large dose of unpleasantness. Make that a very large dose of unpleasantness. To remind me that winning has very little to do with hearing the words "not guilty."

From the first moment I met Davy, I absolutely couldn't stand him. When he eventually fired me I was so relieved. Before I had even met him I had been warned. Three times. Once by his first attorney, whom he fired. Then by his second attorney, whom he also fired, and the third time by the secretary at the public defender office who was searching for a lawyer who could handle him.

"He's a real asshole. No one can put up with him. He already fired Walt and Matt. Julian and Charles have the co-defendants. I'm out of attorneys. If he can't get along with you he's representing himself."

I had a reputation of being able to work with the difficult clients. After clients had fired other lawyers on contract with the public defender, they would end up with me. The previous attorneys would tell me how awful these people were. Uncooperative—*when I go (to jail) to see him all he does is cuss and tell me I'm selling him out. If we didn't meet through the glass he would have hit me.* Unreasonable—*He doesn't have a defense and he won't even consider the plea offer for four years. He'll get twenty if we go to trial.* Ungrateful—*I've found and interviewed all 15 witnesses he told me about. Three of them were out of state and he didn't even have phone numbers. And of course none of them had anything to say that would help him. I've done a Motion to Suppress and a Speedy Trial Motion and still he keeps telling me I'm not doing anything.*

Usually after I have the first appointment with these "problem" clients I don't have any trouble. Sometimes it takes two appointments. I had assumed they would behave with me, and not the others, because I was a woman. This case wouldn't be any different, I wrongly thought, and agreed to take it. The secretary was relieved.

"You should know, he's at the jail now even though he's a pen inmate. He's already destroyed one of the segregation cells there. They may be moving him back to the prison. They don't have the security at the jail to handle someone like him. He's hard core."

I had read the paperwork before I went to see him. He had been in prison for most of his adult life. A series of violent offenses. His current charges were assaults and batteries on peace officers; fighting with prison guards. He was injured. They were injured. The fight took place in the hallway outside of the cafeteria. The witnesses were divided between guards, who all saw *Davy* take the first swing at the guard, and then hit all the other guards who came to help, and other inmates who were looking through the locked glass door from the cafeteria to the hallway. They all saw the *guard* take the first swing and Davy then try to protect himself from that guard and all the others who came to join in the fight.

The Incident Investigator employed by the prison, who is supposed to be impartial, took pictures and did interviews in order to determine what happened and if the guards or the inmates deserved any punishment. There were dozens of pictures of the injuries to the guards. There were two pictures of Davy's injuries. Some of the guards had bruises. Others had bleeding cuts. Every bruise on a guard's face, no matter how small, was photographed from at least three different angles. There was one picture of Davy's face and one of his hands. He had very dark black skin. I couldn't see any bruising on his face but there may have been some. There were some clear scratches across his cheek. His knuckles had little cuts. I knew from previous cases these scratches were from punching. There were no pictures taken of any of the guards' hands.

Each guard had made a written report of the "incident." Each told of being called over their radio by the guard in the control booth to a fight in the hallway outside of the cafeteria. They each saw Davy on top of a guard, beating him. The three or four other guards who came to help described their heroic efforts to pull the crazed Davy from the guard, and Davy, in turn, disabling each rescuer by beating him or her silly with more simultaneous punches and kicks than he had arms and legs with which to deliver.

According to the report Davy had refused to give any more of a statement than he was carrying a cup of ice from the cafeteria to his cell and the guard escorting him tried to stop him, not believing Davy had permission from another guard to do such a thing. When Davy refused to give up the ice the guard began hitting him. Then other guards came and not only was Davy being beaten by the first guard, but by the next three or four who joined in. One guard was a woman and he tried not to hit her, but she was attacking him too and he ended up hitting her in the confusion.

Obviously something happened but I didn't know what. It was probably somewhere between the two extremes described by Davy (I did nothing wrong and the guards did everything wrong) and the guards (we did nothing wrong and Davy did everything wrong). However, the truth didn't matter much. All I was concerned with was what version the State would be able to convince a jury of, and was that version enough to get Davy convicted. It would be an uphill battle for a jury to believe an inmate over a guard. The guards knew that.

Davy was nearly done serving his current ten year sentence. If he won this case he would get out soon. If he lost, he could get up to twenty more years, with a guarantee of at least eight. He was in his early thirties, like me.

I can't remember exactly what was said in our first meeting at the jail, each of us stuffed into matching phone booth sized boxes with a window between us, but it was something like this:

Me: "I'm Sheri, your new attorney."

Him: (holding the phone to his ear, frozen like a statue and looking at me, without a hint of movement in his anger lined face)

Me: (jiggling the switch on the phone as I look at him through the scratched Plexiglas window) "Can you hear me? Is your phone working?"

Him: (motionless but for an unavoidable blink)

Me: "I'm here to talk about your case."

Him: (silence)

Me: "The best way I can help you is if you tell me the truth. Tell me what happened. Anything you tell me is confidential. I won't tell anyone else without your permission. Not the DA, not the police, not the judge."

Him: (silence)

Me: "My job is to help you."

Him: (silence)

Me: (silence)

Him: (silence)

Me: (silence)

Him: (silence)

Me: (putting my pen down, closing my file, and turning slightly to push the buzzer on the door frame behind me to signal to the guard to unlock my door) "Well, I've read all the paperwork. If you don't have anything to tell me then I'll just see you at trial."

Him: "Hey! Where the fuck you going?"

Me: "I've got other clients who actually want to talk to me. I'll go work on their cases."

Him: "What the fuck are they sending me some little fucking white girl who don't know shit. Why the fuck should I talk to you. You're just like those other assholes here to get me to take some plea. I'm not taking nothing! I didn't do shit! They were the ones fucking with me. Those guards were fucking with me."

Me: (Now we're getting somewhere) "Ok. Tell me what happened."

Him: "Why should I tell you shit?"

Me: "So I can see if there's a defense."

Him: "*If* there's a defense? I told you bitch I didn't do shit! I don't need no defense. THEY need the defense. You already think I done it. What the fuck kind of lawyer are you. You don't even look like a lawyer. How old are you? And look at you wearing blue jeans. Aw shit. You like those other assholes. I don't want you. I got a right to a lawyer and I want a different one. A REAL one."

Me: "You have a right to a lawyer period. Not a lawyer you choose. Not a lawyer you like. Just a lawyer. I'm your lawyer and I'm the only one you're getting. The public defender office told me that I'm it. If you fire me your next lawyer is named pro-se."

Him: "Jose? Whose Jose?"

Me: "Not 'Jose,' 'pro-se.' That means you're representing yourself."

Him: (silence)

Me: "I don't need to talk to you to do your case, but it'll probably turn out better if you tell me what happened."

Him: (silence)

Me: "Well it's up to you if you don't want to talk. You're the one facing twenty years. Whatever happens in the end, I go home."

Him: "You gonna make me take some deal?"

Me: "It's my job to tell you about the plea offer. I have to inform you what it says and–"

Him: "See bitch, you gonna sell me out!"

Me: "–it's your decision whether or not to take it."

Him: "–the same as those other fuckers!"

I first started doing criminal law as a full time public defender. At that point I thought part of my job was answering all my client's questions, even if the questions were things like "what the fuck are you gonna' do for me?" Or "How long you been a lawyer? How many trials have you won and how many have you lost? Where are you from? How old are you? Why aren't you married?" I would try my best to remain calm while trying to convince my angry client that I was qualified to defend him, and giving out all sorts of irrelevant personal information. Appointments would go on and on and although I would spend an hour or more in the stuffy meeting room at the jail, I frequently wouldn't get the information I actually needed to work on the case; his rendition of what happened.

The majority of criminal clients behave just fine, even politely. Many times they know they're guilty, they know the state can prove it, and their goals are realistically focused on minimizing the inevitable sentence, not on having me perform some sort of magic to win their case. It is the minority who seem always angry and direct that anger at the only person outside of the jail with whom they have contact; their lawyer.

My boss at the time had been a lawyer for more than twenty years and had done criminal law for much of that time. I walked into his office straight from one of these sorts of visits with a client at the jail. This client had wanted to know why his bond was set so high. He only embezzled some money. Since no one was physically hurt he thought no one should care. Looking at the ugly facts of many of my other cases, I tended to agree. I told him that the prosecutor wanted his bond high because she thought he was a "dangerous criminal" and shouldn't be out on the streets. All he heard was that I called him a dangerous criminal and I spent the next hour trying to explain my comment.

I got back to the office, went straight to my boss's office, dropped my file on the table in front of his fish tank, sat on the table next to the humming filter, and exploded with frustration, retelling the entire discussion I had just endured. When I was finally breathless and exasperated he leaned back in his chair and calmly proceeded to educate me about client control. Unless I enjoyed being locked in a visiting room at the jail and being yelled at by a client, he suggested that I do two things when that starts to happen: 1) say politely "I'm here to talk about your case. If you don't want to talk about your case I'm leaving." And then, if the yelling doesn't stop, 2) leave. It seemed so simple I was embarrassed that I hadn't thought of it on my own.

More times than I can count I have interrupted a tirade of obscenity, or just endless complaining about the unfairness of it all, with the words: "I'm here to talk about your case." Since that meeting with my wise boss I never again allowed myself to be verbally abused by my clients.

Davy was still spewing insults at me.

Me: (gathering up my things again and speaking calmly through the phone to Davy) "I'm here to talk about your case. When you're ready to talk about your case let me know and I'll come back."

I waited a few weeks and didn't get a letter or phone call from him. There was a hearing coming up and it was his opportunity to take the plea offer. The plea offer was for the mandatory eight years and no more. That was far better than losing at trial and getting the entire twenty. I needed to make sure he understood the plea offer and knew what he was risking by rejecting it. Reluctantly I made another appointment to see him.

The second appointment went much like the first except that he asked me about God. More specifically, he demanded to know did I believe in God. He was angry, like before. Most clients ask if I believe they're innocent. I get out of answering the questions by telling them it doesn't matter because I'm not going to be on the jury. I thought this question fell into that same category. I told him that it didn't matter what I believed. He asked me again and clearly wasn't going to stop asking until I answered.

I could have told him what he wanted to hear, yes, and then I knew he would cooperate with me. But I didn't want to lose control. I would answer any question about the law because that was my obligation to him. But to answer a personal question, just because he wants me to, that would be me agreeing that he could control our relationship.

"It doesn't matter if *I* believe in God." I thought quickly how I could avoid answering his question but still gain his cooperation: "What matters" I said slowly, "is if God believes in *you*."

That drew silence. He shook his head slowly as if he was absorbing this philosophical gem I had just deposited in his lap. His face softened. I had passed the test. What religion are you, he asked gently. Jewish, I told him, against my better judgment. He nodded in what I mistakenly thought was approval.

We spent the rest of the meeting talking about what happened that day at the cafeteria. How he had permission about the ice, how the guard didn't believe him, how he pushed him, how he pushed back, how the hallway filled with other guards, being attacked from all sides, doing what he could to protect himself, how he tried to avoid the woman, how she hit his face with her fist, how other inmates were crowded at the window, how they saw, how he's getting ready to get out, finally, and they're doing this to him so he won't. How he hasn't seen his mother in ten years. How he just wants to see his mother.

I told him I would interview all of the guards and talk to the other inmates.

Weeks later, when I had finished all of the interviews I went back to see him. It didn't look good. All of the guards' stories pretty well matched. Whether it was true or not, their testimony would probably convince a jury that Davy had started the fight. He could only claim self defense if he was hit first. The other inmates agreed with Davy's version, but their views of the action were partially obstructed by a turn in the hallway, and each other. Even if the jury believed what the inmates said they saw, it still didn't help Davy that much. The inmate witness who saw the most and whose testimony, if believed, would be the most helpful, went by the name Hitman. It was my job to give Davy my honest evaluation of the case to help him decide whether or not to take the plea offer for eight years, or go to trial and risk losing and getting twenty.

The appointment started out okay until I got into the details of what the guards were saying. Davy got increasingly angry at hearing what they were claiming happened. "He's lying!" or "that's a bunch of bullshit!" he would explode. He wanted the other inmates to have seen more. He was mad at them too, thinking that by being honest about their limited view they were somehow siding with the guards.

He wouldn't consider taking a plea. Everyone was lying. I was on "their" side again, just like the previous attorneys. I didn't know what I was doing. Why would I even talk to him about a plea unless I thought he was guilty. He needed a lawyer who believed in him. How could I defend him if I didn't believe him. It's because I'm Jewish. I just want money and he can't pay me so that's why I'm doing this to him.

I was about to remind him that I was there to talk about his case when he stood up in the little booth, his body nearly filling it, hit the metal shelf with his fist and said "I want somebody else! You're fired Jew Bitch!"

I could handle a client thinking I wasn't a good enough lawyer. Most clients didn't have much to judge by and were understandably worried about their future. The kind of insults that came from the insecurity of being assigned a public defender didn't bother me. When a client would say, "if you were any good you wouldn't be working for the public defender, you would be a real lawyer" I wasn't insulted. I knew that I was good and I knew that working for the pennies the public defender paid was part of my obligation as a lawyer. My obligation to the indigent clients who, just like the rich, shouldn't be wrongly convicted. Plus, the majority of criminal defendants can't afford to pay a lawyer. Poor people tend to get arrested much more often than rich people.

If you like being in the courtroom and having challenging cases, then taking public defender work is the best way to satisfy your goals. I have done far more jury trials than most private attorneys who have only worked for paying clients. My paying clients should personally thank the hundreds of public defender clients who have been unfortunate enough to get themselves arrested. The experience I gained from all of their cases is what has made me the lawyer that the paying clients want.

It didn't bother me that public defender clients misunderstood why I was doing public defender work. But to want to fire me because I was Jewish? Completely different. I didn't for a second feel a need to try to understand that hatred. I knew I wouldn't devote one more second trying to help Davy Rice. He didn't deserve me. Let him get twenty.

I pressed the button to have the door opened, hung up the phone, gathered my papers, and thankfully, the lock on the door clicked open just at that moment. I didn't want to have to look at Davy any longer. I drove straight to the public defender's office and told the secretary I was done. He was representing himself. I submitted to the judge a written Motion to Withdraw as Counsel for the Defendant; *communications have broken down between undersigned counsel and the defendant,* I wrote, *and we no longer have a working attorney client relationship.* Like the two lawyers before me, the judge let me out of the case.

Weeks later another lawyer, a criminal defense attorney, told me that she was in the courtroom when Davy had his next scheduled hearing. He asked the judge if he could represent himself. The judge asked him if he knew how complicated the legal system was, if he knew he would have to follow all the rules at trial just like he was a lawyer, is he sure this is what he wants since he's looking at a lot of time if he loses. Yes, yes and yes, he had answered, and the judge said he could represent himself. Trial was set for two months away.

"He called me a Jew Bitch." I told her.

"Wow. I can't believe he figured out you're Jewish. He seems kind of slow."

"He didn't figure it out, I told him." She opened her eyes wide. She had been doing this work longer than me and was clearly surprised that I would reveal something personal to a client. "My mistake" I admitted.

I wanted to never think about Davy Rice again, but every so often his case would float through my mind. One of the guards said when he came running to help he slipped on the floor just before he got to the spot in the hallway where the fight was happening. He mentioned this to explain why a guard who came into the hallway after him actually got to the fight a few seconds before him. The hallway was shaped like an L with the door to the cafeteria on one end and the door leading to the cells on the other. All the guards rushed in to help through the door leading to the cells. The inmates were gathered behind the door to the cafeteria, looking through a square window. The fight took place mostly near the bend in the L, allowing the inmates to see only parts of it.

During the appointment when we briefly got along, Davy had told me that he started back to his cell with the guard and then, when they were waiting for the hallway door to the cells to be opened, the guard saw Davy's cup had ice in it and told him he couldn't keep it. Davy protested and the guard knocked it out of his hand and then started hitting him. They then moved backwards into the hall, and the other guards filtered in and joined the fight.

The guard said that as soon as the cafeteria door closed behind him and Davy, Davy starting calling the guard names and when the guard told him to stop, Davy challenged him to a fight and took the first swing. The fight eventually made its way further down the hall and was near the corner of the L when the other guards came.

I kept thinking about the ice. When the first blow was exchanged the cup of ice must have been dropped or knocked out of Davy's hand. The guard who slipped after coming in through the door leading to the cells probably slipped on melted ice. The only way that the floor would be wet with melted ice at that end of the hallway was if Davy's version of events was right. And the guard's was wrong. It wasn't much, but it was something. Something to use to convince the jury that they should believe Davy over the guard. They could rely on something that, unlike human beings, couldn't lie; melted ice.

But, the hallway wasn't very long. If the encounter started near the cafeteria door, like the guard said, and Davy threw the cup of ice, or it got knocked out of Davy's hand in the affray, then it could have flown through the air some distance before it landed and started to melt. But there was a bend in the hallway. The ice would have had to rebound off a wall to land around the corner from where it started. It was possible, but unlikely.

But, we don't even know what the guard slipped on. Maybe it wasn't water at all. The first guard had the worst injuries and was bleeding from a cut on his head. Maybe the second guard slipped on blood. I wouldn't want to go back again and ask the guard because maybe he would think it through and say blood just to back up the first guard, even if it was water. Better to leave it open, have the guard tell the jury simply the floor was wet and he slipped, just like he told me. Then, in my closing argument, tell the jury it must have been the melted ice, which would mean it happened how Davy said. By then it's too late for any more testimony to contradict that assumption. But wait, I won't be doing a closing argument since I don't represent him. Why am I still thinking about this?

Davy's case would usually come into my mind during the thirty minute drive between my office and court. I would think about our meetings. Was there something different I could have said to make him like me? Should I have lied; told him he had a great defense and I thought he was going to win? I know that's what he wanted to hear. Our appointments would have been easy then. I would prepare for the case and never hear one more complaint from him. He would cooperate when I needed a question answered, like had the guard already called to the control booth to have the second door opened when he hit you? If he did, the guard in the control booth might have been looking at the monitor of the hallway when the fight started. The only hard part about the case would be the case itself, not putting up with Davy.

But then, when he lost, he would be rightly furious having made decisions about his case based on my lie. Sure it would have been easier for me to lie, but it would have been wrong. The two attorneys before me couldn't get along with him either. And they were men. Christian men. The guy was just an ungrateful jerk. Three people willing to help him and he pushed us all away. I should be happy he's going to get twenty. But the guard slipped near the second door when the ice would have spilled near the first door…

Why did I even care if he liked me or thought I was a good attorney? Why would I want his approval anyway? I didn't hate him because he was black so how dare he hate me because I'm Jewish.

But why did I keep thinking about this? The file is in the drawer in the hall with CLOSED written across the front in black magic marker. I need to close it in my head as well. Anyway, a successful defense would require Davy to testify. To tell the jury what he told me about how it happened. It would never work. The jury would see his uncontrolled anger and be convinced from that alone that he would have seen a chance to beat up a guard and taken it.

Two months later when the judge's secretary called my office and told me to be at the courthouse in an hour, to select a jury on Davy's case, I was furious. Apparently that morning he had tried to follow along while the cases before him went through jury selection. The lawyers asking the room full of potential jurors questions about the presumption of innocence, feelings about burglary, whether anyone in their family had ever been a victim of violence, if they could ever picture themselves carrying a gun in their car, would they be thinking about the school play they would be missing instead of focusing on the evidence. He was trying to take down notes on their answers. Another lawyer at the defense table, the one who had told me the judge was going to let Davy represent himself, there with her own client who had a trial starting the following week, was trying to help him. Every criminal case with this judge going to trial in the next month would pick today from this same jury pool.

Davy's main problem was he couldn't write very well and the

answers came too fast. Finally, with the encouragement of the other attorney, he asked the judge for a lawyer. The judge looked through the file and saw that three of us knew about the case. He asked Davy if he cared which lawyer he appointed. Davy chose me. The other lawyer later told me that he said "I want the Jew Bitch" and the judge quickly figured out he meant me.

Forty-five minutes after the call from the judge's secretary I arrived at the courthouse with Davy's closed file and I wasn't happy. I had spent the whole drive complaining out loud how unfair it was that I was going to have to do this trial. Not only was I about to do a jury selection without having even read the standard questionnaires the prospective jurors filled out, and not only couldn't I believe that I had to keep a smile on my face while I sat next to the guy who told me he didn't want me and insulted me, but my most immediate concern was that I was wearing a flowered sundress and flats; far too casual for a jury selection.

When I walked into the courtroom the jury was still at lunch. The two tables pushed together for the defense, surrounded with too many chairs, was splashed with files, pads, pens, and large pieces of paper with hand drawn charts with squares for each seat, the jurors name scribbled in the square and either notes of what they said, or simply a check mark or an X, depending on how that attorney did it. The clients who weren't in jail were at lunch. Davy and the two other inmates who were charged with accessory to his crimes by cheering him on were at the table, cuffed, and with a bunch of guards sitting behind them.

I walked right up to where Davy was seated, he opened his mouth like he was going to say something and before he could get a word out I stood over him and pointed my finger near his face. All the anger that had been building on the drive to the courthouse exploded out of me. "Don't you talk to me! You just sit there, keep you mouth shut, and let me do my job! You understand?" My face was hot.

He looked up at me and shook his head meekly, like a child being scolded. I was loud and the few other people in the courtroom had stopped talking and were looking at us. I dropped my stack of files on the table next to Davy and dug around in my briefcase for the three pens I would need for jury selection; black for listing the jurors names, blue for writing down their comments, and red for giving them a passing or failing grade.

One of the guards sitting behind Davy spoke to me quietly, almost afraid. "Um. Ma'am?" I looked back at him, my face still red and my lips tight. "I think you want that table" and he pointed to where the prosecutors had their papers laid out.

"Why?" I shot back.

"That's where the other DA's are sitting."

"What are you talking about? I'm not a prosecutor." I pointed to Davy. "I'm his attorney."

He looked at Davy and tilted his head sympathetically.

Davy sat dutifully quiet as I got myself ready for return of the jury in the next few minutes. I asked one of the other lawyers how many more cases before mine. Two. Since there are two codefendants the two other lawyers and I will all ask questions in a row, and then meet privately to decide whom to exclude. It will take the time of three cases instead of one. I was told the judge had already commented that we may start tomorrow morning instead of doing half this afternoon and then the other half tomorrow. And that's how it turned out.

For the rest of the day I sat next to a quiet Davy and took notes on the jurors' comments to the other lawyers. When jury selection ended for the day and the guard was about to walk Davy out of the courtroom to the holding cell, he asked me if I needed to talk to him first. I looked only at the guard and shook my head no.

The day long delay had allowed me to read the jury questionnaires in the evening and dress properly. A short black skirt, bright pink silk shirt and black blazer. A double strand pearl necklace, pearl and gold earrings, and bright pink lipstick. I was wearing the gold Citizen watch I treated myself to when I finished my first jury trial years earlier. It wasn't the most expensive one at the jewelry store in the mall, but it was more than the Timex I was wearing, looked nice, and it made me feel like a "real" lawyer. With my well fitted jacket and skirt, classic jewelry, and bright colors, Davy's jury would notice me. They would think I was a lawyer worth listening to and I would rely on this perception the whole trial.

When I walked into the courtroom Davy was already there along with the other two inmates he was charged with. They were all wearing the same pale green button shirt and dark green chino pants. It wouldn't necessarily have looked like prison clothes if they all three hadn't been dressed in it and sitting at the same table. The room was calmer today. Our case was the only one left for jury selection. The second table that had been brought up for the defense had been removed. There was an empty chair between each inmate for his lawyer. I sat in the empty chair next to Davy. We looked at each other. I didn't smile.

"You smell nice" he ventured cautiously after I had looked away, testing to see if I would yell like yesterday.

I was wearing Ysatis perfume and he was right, it did smell nice.

I didn't raise my voice but I didn't say "thank you" either, just paused to let him know I wouldn't be answering. "Your job is to look innocent. Everything else is my job."

"Yes Ma'am."

There was no more talking between us.

The jury was brought in. The judge introduced the case and read the charges. I watched the faces of the jurors as they heard 'Battery on a Peace Officer, four counts, Assault on a Peace Officer, four counts.' Not nearly as bad as 'Criminal Sexual Penetration of a Minor' or 'Attempted Murder.' I always hope that there's a defendant at jury selection who has worse charges than my client so my guy can look good by comparison. The times when *I've* had that worse client have been painful.

The other two defense lawyers and I stood up in turn and the jury had to say whether any of them knew us. Then the defendants stood up. Same question. Then the prosecutor questioned the jury.

Can you be fair, yes or no. A dull hum of a "yes." The sixty potential jurors were bored, having answered these same questions all day yesterday and never hearing anything interesting, despite all the cases being criminal.

Do you have any prejudice against the DA's office, yes or no. A dull hum of a "no." Many in the group weren't bothering to answer at all.

Do you have any prejudice against the police, yes or no.

Have any of you been a victim of a battery, yes or no.

Do any of you have close family members who work at the prison, yes or no. A few hands go up.

Would the fact that your nephew works at the prison as a guard make it more likely you would believe the guards in this case, yes or no (No. It would have no effect at all. Just because I know how hard it is for him at work and what those people are like, well, I guess you call them 'prisoners.' Just because I know what those 'prisoners' are like and what the guards have to put up with, I can be fair to both sides. I would be honored to be on this jury. I would consider it my duty to my nephew).

The prosecutor is done and the judge takes a short break. The two other defense attorneys and I decide who will go first. My client has the most serious charges so the others agree I can decide the order. I choose to go last. The jury will pay attention better if they know they get to leave when I'm done.

I know that the jury is going to hate Davy and his friends because they're in prison. I want to deal with this right away.

Me: "So Ms. ### take a look at Mr. Rice and tell me what you think." I stand next to Davy and put my hand on his shoulder.

Ms. ###: "Oh, I don't know. I don't really know him. He's okay I guess." She's looking down so that I'll stop talking to her.

Me: "And Mr. ###. What do you think? Take a look at Mr. Rice and tell me what you think?"

Mr. ###: "What do you mean." Uncomfortable. "He looks like a nice gentleman."

Me: "And Mrs. ###. What do you think?"

Mrs. ###: "Well, he seems fine." Answer quickly and maybe she won't keep asking me questions.

Me: "Really? He seems fine? Do you have a daughter?"

Mrs. ###: "Yes. Two. They're grown."

Me: "Well, let's say one of them brings Davy home to dinner for you to meet. He's her new boyfriend. What do you think now?"

Mrs. ###: This is an older white woman, who would likely be horrified if her daughter brought home this big black convict. She stumbles for words. "Ahh. Well, he seems... it would be up to my daughter... My husband would..."

Me: "You'd be surprised, right?"

Mrs. ###: She breathes a loud sigh of relief "yes."

Me: "First off because he's black. You wouldn't expect your daughter to date someone black. Right? It's okay. I just want to know the truth."

Mrs. ###: "Well, yes."

Me: "And he's wearing some sort of religious hat on his head" and I point to the colorful Muslim cap he's wearing. "You would wonder what that's about, wouldn't you?"

Mrs. ###: "Yes, I would." Other jurors are shaking their heads in agreement.

And I call on another, and then another, asking each one to confirm that they would react negatively if Davy was brought home to dinner. Nearly half the jury pool was happily agreeing that every detail I pointed out about Davy gave them legitimate cause to be even more wary of him. The room was full of polite hate. Then, it happened. It took a little longer than I thought, but then the juror's hand went up. I didn't know which one it would be, exactly, but I knew the juror would be there somewhere.

Me: I point to her. "Yes Ma'am. Do you agree with what these other people are saying?"

Ms. ###: "No. I disagree completely! This is just terrible."

Me: "What do you mean? Disagree how?"

Ms. ###: "I don't know anything about him. I've just seen him. You can't judge a book by its cover. It's true I might be surprised when I first saw him because he was black, I'm only being honest, but that would only be for a minute. If my daughter was interested in him I would want to know who he was, talk to him, see where he's from, what he does, what's his family like. It's unfair to judge someone by looks. I can't believe you're even asking us to do that. Aren't you supposed to be his lawyer? Aren't you supposed to be helping him?"

Another hand: "Yeah, you're already getting us not to like him. We don't even know what happened."

Me: "Well, he's in prison already. You know he did a crime at some point to get there? Isn't that enough for you?"

Many hands shoot up. I call on them all in turn. I don't even have to ask questions. They start speaking as soon as I point.

When you make assumptions you're almost always wrong.

Everybody deserves a chance.

People can change.

The past is the past.

I wouldn't want someone to judge me by my looks.

I don't care if he's a prisoner, that doesn't make him a bad person, just someone who did something bad.

Some people are wrongly convicted you know. Did they have DNA the first time? Do they have DNA now?

Honestly I don't know many black people and I probably have some wrong ideas. I would try even harder *not* to judge him because of that.

He's innocent until proven guilty isn't he?

Me: "How many of you agree with that? That right now he is innocent?" Every hand goes up.

Me: "Who decides if he's guilty?"

"We do" the group answers with gusto.

Me: "And how do you decide?"

Some hands are up, some people are just talking out. I pick a hand. Mr. ###: "How do you decide if he's guilty?"

Mr. ###: "That's what this trial's about. I have to hear the evidence. I don't know yet but I'll know when it's done."

Me: "What if you hear all the evidence and you're not convinced he did it? Then how do you have to vote?"

Mr. ###: Short pause. "Not guilty?" He asks.

Me: "Yes. The law says that if at the end of the trial you're not really,

really convinced he did it, then you have to vote not guilty. Anyone have a question about that?" Silence.

Me: "So, let me ask you all, if you get all of the evidence in this trial, you hear from all of the witnesses, see all of the exhibits, and still you're not convinced that he did it, how do you vote?"

Group: "Not guilty" they all call out.

So far Davy's winning.

I walk back to the table and sit next to Davy. The judge excuses the jury and tells them we will reconvene in half an hour and let them know who has been selected. We all stand as the jury walks out.

Immediately after the door closes the other attorneys and I, all friends, lean into the table and start going through the juror's names seeing if we agree on who to keep and who to exclude. I can feel Davy staring at me. I don't even want to look at him. He won't stop and it's distracting. I push my seat back a bit and turn towards him.

"What" I say. His mouth is open and the angry lines on his face are gone. He seems smaller. "What is it already!" My voice is quick and sharp. "We need to get this done and the judge isn't going to give us endless time."

Davy: Silence, and then, "You're gonna help me?"

Me: Impatiently. "Yes! That's my job. I've only told you that about ten times."

Davy: "I know. But you're really gonna try to help me." Not a question, but a statement. He's speaking slowly and softly. He's amazed. He's different. There are only inches between my face and his because of how we are sitting. It's like we are alone. I forget about the other attorneys at the table, the two other defendants, the pack of guards standing behind us all.

Me: "Yes" I say quietly. I look into his face. The hate is gone. I can tell he will never yell at me again. I speak slowly and look right into his eyes. "Yes. I'm going to help you." It's like he's hearing me say this for the first time. Actually, no. It's not that. It's like he's heard me say it before, but this is the first time he's *believing* it.

Davy: "And you're good." Again, a statement.

Me: "Yes. I'm going to help you. And yes. I'm good."

Davy sits back in his chair looking at me. A smile starts to stretch the corners of his mouth. He's nodding his head gently up and down. "Allll riiiight" he says quietly, ending the drawn out words with a final nod of his head.

It is at this moment I realize that Davy needed to experience me helping him in order to believe it would happen. That people have probably promised him a lot throughout his life but never kept their promises. I understood that all the yelling and anger he showed me was really meant for those other people. The one's who said they would help but didn't. There was nothing I could have done or said to get to this point of trust sooner. He would only trust me when I proved to him that he should. I knew exactly why he called me a Jew Bitch, and I quickly forgave him.

The trial took three days. Each morning he would ask if I slept okay. Tell me how nice I looked. Pour me a glass of water from the pitcher on the table. Remind me to ask him if I needed to know something about that day. About how the hallway looked. About how the food line works. The gossip about the guards. Anything.

During the breaks I would tell him how the testimony of the previous witness hurt or helped. How I didn't ask this guard how the battery chargers for the radios worked, but would ask the next guard. How in my interview with the next guard he emphasized how important a charged radio was. A guard's "life line," he had said. How the first thing he does when he goes on shift is check the battery in his radio. When he's on duty it's his "only weapon." I wanted the jury to hear those words. The guard who claimed that Davy hit him first was carrying a radio with a dead battery. It didn't make any difference for the case, but I wanted the jury to think he was lazy, poorly trained, didn't take his job seriously. Was the kind of person who would lie. Davy shook his head in agreement. "You're the boss" I heard then, and over and over.

I had told Davy not to talk to me while witnesses were testifying because I needed to listen. He should wait for a break. Mostly he remembered, but when the woman guard was testifying he started to whisper in my ear. I shook my head no. He tapped me on the shoulder. I pointed to the pad of paper and pen on the table. She was testifying to the same story she told me in the interview. She was called to the fight. Came in and saw Davy on top of the guard beating him. She helped to pull him off. Maybe got the back of his shirt. Definitely didn't hit him. And then, for no reason at all, he took a swing at her. Punched her. She was little and some of the jurors gasped at the image she created. Hitting the male guards for no reason is one thing, but hitting a woman. They couldn't wait to convict him.

As I took speedy notes of her testimony almost as fast as she was talking, Davy slowly wrote something out on the pad and then slid it over to me. It said, "ringss skrached my face." I looked up to the witness stand. Her hands were folded neatly on top of the copies of her reports that sat on the small ledge in front of her. She had rings on both hands. A wedding ring with the diamond held above her finger by long prongs, and what looked like a clump of small rubies on the other hand. Probably her birth stone. They were also set in prongs.

Years before, when my husband had presented me with an engagement ring the round diamond was set away from the ring with prongs. After a few months I realized it was going to be a problem. When I was doing my medical work the latex glove would catch on the protruding stone and tear. And even if I could carefully get the glove over it intact, I certainly couldn't do an internal exam with that hand because the woman would get poked by the ring. Eventually I had the ring changed to a bezel setting; the back of the diamond lying flat against the finger with a smooth loop of gold around it.

If the guard had hit Davy in the face, like he claimed, her rings would have scratched him. Just like the scratches on his cheek that were shown in the picture.

My cross examination took less than five minutes.

"Ma'am are you wearing any rings today?"

"Yes" she looks down at her hands and giggles a little at the easy question.

"Were you wearing those rings on the day of the incident?"

"Yes. I always wear these rings."

"Your honor, may the witness step down and show her hands to the jury?"

The judge raises his eyebrows and stares at me, but can't think of a reason to say no. "You want her to show her hands to the jury?"

"Yes. Specifically, her rings."

She walks slowly in front of the jury box, hands outstretched, palms down. She giggles a little at the informality, and so do a few of the jurors, but each juror looked over the divider at her hands.

It would be two more days until it came up again, in my closing argument. I talked all about the ice. Where it would have dropped and melted. Where the guard slipped. How it only made sense if it happened Davy's way. And all the other problems with the State's case. How Davy was getting out. How he would never risk an incident that would keep him there any longer. And then, the final thought. What some high priced jury consultants claim is all that the jury will remember; the last thing that is said.

"Remember the female guard? She said she never hit Davy. She took an oath and swore to tell you the truth and said she never hit Davy. That he was hitting her. That he was hitting everyone. That he started it. All the guards said that." They shook their heads in acknowledgement. "And then Davy told you something different. He told you the guard attacked *him*. That he was defending himself, just like the law says he can. They can't both be right; the guards and Davy. And whose telling the truth is the difference between guilty and not-guilty." Again, some head shook up and down.

Then I held up the picture of Davy's face and asked them to look hard at his cheeks. That they would see little scratches. They craned their necks to see. I assured them that they would have the picture in the jury room and could look at it all they wanted, but I was sure they would see the same scratches I did. "And remember when the guard walked in front of you and showed you her hands." Some of them shook their heads up and down. "It probably didn't make much sense at the time. But remember her rings? How they stuck out?" Some more head shaking.

I pause and take a few steps back and to the side until I am standing directly in front of the jury box. I move the picture to my left hand and make a first with my right. I don't say a word as I slowly rake my fist across my cheek, turning my head in response to the demonstrative blow. Then I hold up the picture of Davy's scratched cheek. I don't have to say anything. They all understand.

Now, at the end of the three day trial, when we are ordered to stand as the jury is getting up to leave the courtroom, having just delivered their not-guilty verdict, Davy was sweet and polite, like a little kid unable to contain his giddiness while looking over his still wrapped birthday presents. He was absolutely overtaken with amazement that twelve strangers would care about anything that had to do with him.

"Can I thank them?" he leaned down and whispered in my ear. No one had ever asked me that before.

"Yes."

As the bailiff leads the twelve white and Hispanic men and women past the front of the defense table on their way out of the courtroom, Davy, in his green prison shirt and pants, ankles chained together so he can't do more than shuffle when he walks, and a bracelet around his wrist that will deliver an electrical shock strong enough to drop him to the floor if the guard behind him pushes the button on the remote control, smiles broadly and says "thank you" to each juror who passes by.

A few of the jurors turn to look at him. One, a middle aged white woman with red hair, whom for the past three days Davy referred to as "red," smiles warmly at him. During jury selection we learned that she was a volunteer for a literacy program at the prison to teach inmates to read. At the end of the second day of trial Davy had said that he was looking forward to her teaching him; she looked friendly and he wanted the social contact.

"She's not going to teach you" I had responded.

He looked at me with confusion. "Why not?"

"Because you're not going to be in prison." He smiled at my hopefulness.

It was hard to believe that this man I was joking so easily with had fired me just a few weeks before. Called me a Jew Bitch. Told me that he didn't believe that I would help him and I was just like the rest of them. That he was a Muslim and that was why I wouldn't help him. That he was black and that was why I wouldn't help him. That he was in prison and that's why I wouldn't help him. That the public defender wasn't paying me much so that's why I wouldn't help him. That it was easier for me to do nothing than prepare for his case so that's why I wouldn't help him. That no one would care if I let a convicted felon get convicted again so that's why I wouldn't help him. That I got my money from the state, just like the prosecutor, so that's why I wouldn't help him. And he was right to worry.

Those were indeed all reasons why I might not help him. But for reasons he couldn't name, reasons he couldn't imagine, reasons that didn't make any logical sense, I helped him anyway. I had to. That was my job. That's a lawyer's obligation to a client. The law says every defendant whose sentence could be incarceration is entitled to a lawyer. I was defending the Constitution by defending him. This was what all criminal defense lawyers say when someone at a dinner party gasps "how can you defend those people?" Those reasons were all true, but they weren't the reasons I helped him. I had helped him because I was all he had, and it would be wrong to let him down. I was motivated by selflessness, I proudly thought.

Not much later I found out that I wasn't so selfless after all. I wasn't helping him out of the goodness of my heart or out of loyal adherence to the oath I took as a lawyer. I didn't know it at the time, but the reason I helped him was for the feeling I got when I read his letter.

It came only a few weeks after the trial. The small, deliberate, printed letters were almost painful to look at. Upper and lower case mixed at random. Even thought it was short, only one paragraph, I could tell it had taken him a lot of time to write.

I skimmed over most of the letter reading the basic *thank you's* that are certainly nice to hear, but aren't anything unusual. Especially following a win. I was more touched by the effort that I knew he put into the letter than what I imagined would be the specific contents. But one line, tucked inartfully between the 'I didn't like you at the beginning' part, and the 'such a good closing argument you should be an actress' part, was the line that I realized had been the reason I helped him. The pay I didn't even know was coming and couldn't have expected. I no longer remember the misspellings or punctuation errors because I don't remember the words as they looked on the paper, but instead I hear Davy saying them.

'Only three people have ever helped me my whole life: my mother, Jesus, and you.'

I have since moved offices four times, twice to bigger and better locations, and unintentionally a third and fourth time, to and from a temporary space after the Probation and Parole Department that was located in my same office building, was set on fire one night. At the end of every year I have all the documents in case files over seven years old removed and shredded. I have shifted and re-sorted the papers in my seemingly endless stacks and baskets more times than I can count in optimistic efforts to become better organized. Through all of this, not surprisingly, I lost the letter. But I will never lose the memory of that line. I smile when I think of him calling me a Jew Bitch. I shake my head at how ridiculous that comment, and the hatred behind it, turned out to be. I imagine he does the same thing.

4

The Dead Cow

I woke up just before six o'clock to my Rottweiler, Gnasher, tugging at the covers on the bed, his big toothy mouth gripping a ball of white comforter I got at the discount store. The stamped pattern of little blue flowers looked slightly smudged. Gnasher was standing on the old stretched out sweatshirt I wore every morning on the walk. He must have carried it in his mouth from the pile on the other side of the room and then dropped it to get the blankets. As soon as I said "quit it" to Gnasher, the other three dogs came running in the bedroom wagging and barking at the realization that I was awake and they would be going on a walk soon.

I had checked my court calendar the night before and knew my first hearing was at nine o'clock. If I left in the next fifteen minutes I would back with enough time to shower, put on stockings, jewelry and mascara, and get to court in Taos in time to say hello to my client before his case was called. This was the day before the dead cow, but I didn't know it yet.

I pulled on the sweat pants and t-shirt I had worn the day before, and the day before that, and then retrieved the sweatshirt from half under the bed and put it on too. The dogs were running around in circles as I sat on the couch and put on my sneakers.

This dark windy morning we all piled in the front of the pick up and drove into the rising sun the mile across the highway to the endless acres of scrub brush covered hills. This was our weekend truck. The battered one you see in front of every other house on my road that is used mostly for hauling trash to the dump and bringing the new refrigerator home from Sears. Only in an extreme emergency would you ever been seen in such a truck during the week. Mine has a big crack in the windshield, the passenger side window is permanently down, and the tailgate opens only after performing a complicated ritual involving two sets of pliers, wire, and a broken wooden spoon. The dogs heads are jammed out the windows and tails bang against every surface with loud thwacks.

As soon as I stop the truck two dogs jump out the open window. The other two run across my lap out my open door. There are miles of trails snaking through the dirt, mostly from people driving around on ATV's. After ten minutes of walking I could no longer hear the noise of the highway. The trails spread out over small round hills, flat valleys in between. I knew I would stop to enjoy a moment of shade exactly three times in the next hour; once under each of the three well spaced trees we would encounter on the long trail.

The dogs would run up and down the hills, chasing rabbits and sniffing in the low dry bushes and cactus, and also keeping a watchful eye on me as I walked predictably on the trail. The land was officially maintained by the Bureau of Land Management, but mostly it was ignored. For the past few weeks I was careful to look ahead on the trail for small herds of cows. This was calving season and I didn't want the dogs playfully chasing after pregnant cows. I was four months pregnant myself, and although walking felt great, the thought of being scared and chased did not seem very appealing. I assumed the pregnant cows felt the same way.

I am about half way through my usual route, walking across the top of a series of small hills. Down in the valley to my left there were some cows wandering around. Ranchers would lease this land for their cattle. They were supposed to come once a day to leave food and check on the animals. I had never seen anyone doing either. The cows in the valley were pretty far off. I couldn't make out the individual cows, but just saw the movement of the group. I heard mooing every so often. The dogs were on the top of the hill with me and we would soon be past the cows below. The cows were farther away from me than I thought the dogs would wander so I didn't bother changing paths.

As I walked, the dogs sniffing around my feet, I heard a different kind of mooing; a long slow moo. It seemed one cow was mooing until she was out of breath. Then there would be a pause, and a long slow moo again. The sound was coming from the exact same spot every time. I stopped on the top of the hill and squinted against the brightening sun. I could see a group of cows moving around, but off to the side was what looked like one cow, not moving. I couldn't make out any detail. She must be injured.

Occasionally I would see coyotes run across the hills and I guess this cow had been attacked. She was hurt. Dying. It was my immediate instinct to go down and look, see if there was anything I could do. But then the dogs would follow me, I thought. They would bark and run and maybe even attack the hurt cow; the last thing she needed.

I stood on the hill trying to decide whether I should figure out a way to go to the cow, or just keep walking. I knew I should go help her, I felt it. Or at least just be with her, but because of the dogs I tried to talk myself out of it. If I went to her there was nothing I was going to be able to do for her anyway, I told myself. I should let nature take its course. That me seeing the bleeding wounds from the coyote attack wouldn't make it any better, it would just satisfy my curiosity; rubbernecking at the scene of a cow accident. And I knew for sure the carrying on of the dogs would only make the death more frightening for the hurt cow. I listened to the mooing for a few minutes more and then forced myself to start walking. Eventually I couldn't hear it anymore, but I was still thinking about it. All the way back to the car I tried to convince myself I had done the right thing by leaving.

All day and into the night I worried about the cow. I imagined what I could do: go back without the dogs and bring a bottle of water and a dish, open my midwife bag and get antiseptic, sterile water, and suture packs to clean and close her wounds. Maybe it was just a painful infection. I could coat it with the erythromycin cream I put in the newborn's eyes. I could bring IV supplies. Replace the blood loss with lactated ringers. Starting the IV would be easy, cow veins must be huge. I would keep putting in fluids until her heart rate normalized. But how fast should I set the drip? And what's a normal cow heart rate anyway? Where exactly do I put the stethoscope to listen for it? I couldn't carry a stand for the IV bag all the way out there so I would just have to hold the bag above her all the while as it slowly emptied.

I tried to stop my racing thoughts. I should just call my vet who takes care of the dogs. But how would I get the cow to the office? I couldn't. She would have to come to the cow. I could give her directions, meet her at the turn off and we could walk back to the cow together. Carrying her equipment. The more I thought about it the more it seemed, at the least, to be ridiculous, and at the most, to be unrealistic. Besides, nature has its own plan.

After a dozen years as a home birth midwife I had learned that was true. The less you interfere the more smoothly it goes; the labor that's induced is longer and more painful than the labor that starts naturally. This was the difference between being a lawyer and a midwife; as a lawyer I had to make "it" happen, as a midwife I had only to watch, and "it" happened on its own. The best thing I could to help the cow was to leave her alone.

The next morning the dogs and I set out as usual. I was eager to get back to the spot. The dogs were oblivious to my faster pace as they zigzagged across the trail, sniffing and wagging. I hoped that I would see an empty spot in the field below the path and know that the cow had healed and trotted off to join the other cows. As I got closer I heard nothing but the jingling dog collars around me. I was hopeful that I would see nothing as well. I came around a corner and got a view of the valley, I could see the dark patch where the brown cow still lay. So she had died after all. I was instantly sad. Though I told myself that it was as nature had intended, that I wouldn't have know how to help even if I had tried, no matter how hard I tried, I couldn't convince myself I had done nothing wrong by this cow.

I edged myself slowly down the hill sideways. Every few steps dirt rolled out from under my feet. I didn't worry about hurting myself, but all through my pregnancy I was aware of my belly, taking care of it like it was a big bowl of soup that I was driving around, trying to keep from spilling on the seat next to me.

Picking my way gingerly down the hill, I could see the cow coming into focus ahead of me. She was on her side, I couldn't tell whether I was walking towards her head or her rear. The dogs were bounding ahead and nearly to the bottom of the hill. I inched my way to the flat ground. The dogs were wandering in circles around the cow, noses to the ground, and were uncharacteristically quiet. They were blocking my view and I could see only scattered pieces of the cow—a leg, a section of back—and my mind was starting to put them together. Finally, I got an unblocked look straight in front of me. The head. The cow was lying with its head closest to me, its long body trailing into the distance, absolutely motionless. Indeed, she was dead.

I slowed down. Although I wanted to see, I suddenly thought I shouldn't be looking, that what I assumed was her death was private, solemn. I walked a few more steps and then gasped. My hand flew over my mouth. I couldn't move. At the far end of the cow there was another head, the head of her dead calf, its body only half out. The cow had died giving birth. Her calf got stuck and there was no one to help her get it out. Well, almost no one.

I forced myself to walk closer. I stood at the middle of the cow, near her stiff legs, moving my gaze between the two heads. The calf's head and its two front legs were out, the back two still inside. One of the legs was no doubt bent in an odd position preventing it from fitting through the mother's bones.

With human babies it's the shoulder that gets stuck. When it does, I reach in, move it to one side of the pubic bone, and the baby comes out. I could have reached my hand inside the cow, felt for the leg and moved it around whatever bone it was stuck behind. It probably would have taken just a short time for me to get oriented and make the correction. Two minutes at most. The mother would have let me do it even though it would have been uncomfortable, sensing, like any mother, that I was helping. But I wouldn't have that chance. Now they both were dead.

I sat on the ground and the dogs immediately came over and started licking the tears off my face. My mind turned over the possibilities, now irrelevant. The calf might have already died from the long labor before I got there, or maybe it had died sometime before the labor even started, the stillborn triggering labor to start. Maybe I couldn't have done anything for the calf, but still I could have helped the mother. I looked into her face. The side that was up showed her large brown eye, still open. I walked around to her front and crouched in front of her nose to see the underside of her head. The other eye was open as well. I stayed crouched down next to the cow's head until my legs ached from the position, then I sat down in the dirt. Eventually the dogs and I finished the walk.

While I was getting dressed I told my husband. When I was standing outside of the courtroom I told my client. When the judge took a fifteen minute break, I told the attorney I was against. I told nearly everyone I saw that day and the next, whether they were interested or not. I told them all about the dead cow and my shamefully inadequate efforts.

For days the things I could have done for the cow, should have done for the cow, played prominently in my mind, uncontrollably interrupting my other thoughts. Then from not being able to stop talking about it, I shifted to not being able to talk about it. The words I needed to describe my feelings just didn't seem to exist. Within a week I had taken to following my husband's annoyed request to quit going on about it already.

It was a few years later and I had nearly stopped thinking about the dead cow. At some point I forced myself to make a final deliberate effort to make peace with the whole situation. I had firmly told myself that the there was nothing I could have done for the cow, and I wasn't responsible for her anyway. I am not responsible for the whole world, I sternly lectured myself, that's God's job. But a few years later when I was spending the day observing in a high risk obstetric unit, the dead cow came to me for one last time.

I had a long blue gown on over my scrubs. My shoes were covered with blue booties. I tied a flat blue cap over my pulled back hair, put a cloth mask over my mouth and nose and tied it both behind my ears and on top of my head. I followed the nurse I'd been trailing into the delivery room and we both put on sterile gloves. I wasn't used to this formality. I felt as much like a stranger in this hospital as most of the patients did.

I usually go to home births wearing my regular clothes. Sometimes a silk blouse, pencil skirt and heels depending on when the call comes. When the mother starts pushing I put on a bright blue and green plaid cooking apron I got at the Dänsk factory outlet store in Santa Fe. I liked it because it had deep pockets in the front that would be perfect for stashing a stethoscope, a pen, and an emergency pair of gloves. It also keeps blood and amniotic fluid from splashing on my clothes. I wash it after every birth and keep it in my birth bag with my instruments.

Everyone in this delivery room, and there were seven of us, were dressed exactly alike; covered in blue. The gurney, where the mother was lying flat on her back with her legs apart and held up by stirrups, was the focus of the room. Except for a square gap in the middle of her legs, the mother was covered in blue cloth too. Her vagina was stained brown with betadine. Blood from the already cut episiotomy dripped down into a small silver bowl, making a soft 'ping' with every drop. I stood in the far corner with my nurse, next to the resuscitation station and the two pediatricians. Ahead of me there was a woman sitting on a stool in front of the brown and red square; the doctor who would be delivering the baby. The mother couldn't see the doctor and the doctor couldn't see her.

The doctor on the stool was looking at the monitor off to the side and when the graph lines would rise, indicating a contraction, the doctor would tell the mother to push. She counted to ten as part of her pushing command. Although the doctor was directing her voice where she was looking, into the mother's vagina, it must have floated up. The mother looked like she was giving a weak push in response. I quietly asked the pediatrician what was wrong with this baby, why was this delivery high risk? He answered loudly.

"Meconium. So far it looks thin. We won't even suction it if it isn't thick."

"I thought you were supposed to suction all meconium, even if it's light. That's what I was taught." I kept my voice down, hoping that he would respond in kind.

"Used to be that way." Loud as before. "Now we only suction if it's thick. That's what the new research says."

I shook my head. I was used to being quiet at births. Talking only to encourage the mother.

The doctor on the stool was counting again. The mother was flat on her back and I knew the pushing would be more effective, get the baby out sooner, if she could sit up a little and gravity could help the baby move down. If I was doing the delivery I would have pillows behind the mother, propping her up to more of a sitting position. I didn't want to get in trouble by interfering, but I didn't want the mother to have to go through twice as many painful contractions than she would if she was more upright. I walked across the large room to the side of the mother's bed. I'm sure everyone thought I was a nurse, not a home birth midwife getting her re-certification hours.

To my surprise there was someone standing across from me. A short man, also in a mask and gown. He had been blocked from my view by the sheets draped over the mother's bent knees. He was standing stiffly still with the mother's hand in his. This must be the father. He was silent. I looked down at the mother's face. Tears were coming from the corners of her eyes. She looked at me, able to see only my eyes because of my mask. She looked alone and terrified. She had long dark hair, dark skin, and brown eyes. Hispanic. Maybe around twenty. She couldn't see anyone except her husband. The doctor and nurses between her legs were miles away, her baby off with them. I knew I was going to help her. That I was supposed to help her.

I took her hand in mine and said, "My name is Sheri. I'm going to help you." I smiled under my mask. In response, she gave me a blank look.

I tried again. "*Mi nombre es Sheri. Voy a ayudarte.*" She and her husband looked at each other and then at me, and smiled with relief. Six other people in the room and I'm the only one who speaks Spanish. We are in the largest hospital in the largest city in a state with one of the largest Spanish speaking populations in the country. My being in the room is practically an accident. Or so it would seem.

The nurses standing at the mother's knees looked at me. The doctor on the stool looked out from under a leg. She stopped counting and telling the mother to push. It was my job now. I pulled down my mask a little with my free hand and smiled at the mother. I whispered conspiratorially, "*Estoy partera.*" I'm a midwife. The mother grasped my hand hard, shook her head up and down, and looked right into my eyes.

With the next contraction I put my hand behind her back and sat her up, my other hand still holding hers. "*Cuando tiene ganas, empuje!*" When you have the urge, push! She looks at me and pushes. "*Bien hecho!*" Good work, I say and I shake my head encouragingly. The contraction is over and I lay her down. I tell her to relax and take slow deep breaths. I am looking into her brown eyes and she into my blue. She is trying to slow her breathing down to match mine as I exaggerate slow breaths in and out, just inches from her face. She can't feel the air I'm blowing because of my mask, but she can hear me blowing. Another contraction and I sit her up again and she pushes. In no time I can start to see the top of the baby's head and I tell her so.

That's right.

Just like that.

You're moving the baby down.

Good work!

Is the urge gone? Then take a break. Breathe with me.

We are blowing on each other's faces again. Then up for the next push.

"*La cabecita esta aqui!*" The little head is here!

"*Papa, mira!*" Daddy, look! I tilt my head towards the baby. The father cautiously peers over his wife's legs and sees the head come out. He leans down and kisses her forehead through his mask.

Push again for the body!

The baby comes out into the doctor's hands. I put my finger to my mouth to let the parents know to be quiet. Their voices could stimulate the baby to breathe before the pediatrician can suction the meconium out of the throat.

One of the nurses immediately cuts the cord and brings the baby across the room to the warming table behind the pediatrician. His back is to us, blocking the view of the baby. He, the other pediatrician, and my nurse are huddled around the little table working. After about a minute there is a cry. The mother and father look at me, unsure. I shake my head up and down, indicating that the baby is okay, giving them permission to be happy. They relax.

The nurse I am shadowing is leaving and motioning for me to go with her. The baby doesn't need to come with us to the newborn ICU after all. "*Felicidades.*" Congratulations, I say in preparation for leaving the bedside. I look into her eyes. In that moment I see the eyes of the cow. Everything stops.

I am sitting on the ground next to her head, feeling empty with failure. My eyes are overflowing with tears as I tell her she was brave, that she had done everything she could, that it wasn't her fault. That she tried her hardest and when she had pushed for the final futile time, she did the last thing she could think of; she asked for help. She hung on until she saw someone walking, and then, with the little strength she had left, knowing that her calf had already died, but hoping that maybe she could live to mourn it properly, she called out for help. And how fortunate she was that it was me she was calling to. A midwife. Someone who actually knew how to help. Someone who wanted to help. Someone with her own baby inside who surely would understand.

I got close to her still face, her open eyes. I wanted her to see that I had come after all. That I had heard her plea. That she didn't struggle without a reason. That she was right to ask. That it wasn't she who failed her calf, it was I who failed her. I assured her that some good would come from her tragedy. My mistake.

The new mother squeezes my gloved hand, breaking me out of my trance. "*Gracias*" she whispers. I look into her eyes; her fear is gone as if it has floated far away. So distant she can hardly believe it was so recently part of her. Something has floated out of me too. Just disappeared into the air.

I see the big brown eyes of the cow framed by their long, curled lashes. They are no longer stuck in the pain of that last frozen push. They are relaxed. She and her calf are together. Finally at peace. Smiling. Happy. And so am I.

5

Max

"Can I help you." The prison guard is making more of a statement than actually asking me a question. He says this all day long.

"I'm a lawyer. I have an appointment to see a client." He takes my driver's license and gray plastic Bar identification card and stands next to my open window, copying information down onto the paper on his clipboard.

He returns my identification by holding it out in front of him at his waist, not doing me any favors. I don't know if it's because I'm on the defense side, which he sees as against the police, or just because he's sick of his job. I reach out my window and stretch my arm out all the way to take it back.

"Minimum or Maximum?"

"Max." I say. He starts to point up the hill. "I know the way." I drive through the gap between the oversized stop signs out of the right side of the rotary, towards the hill. At the top of the traffic circle, just to my left, is the Old Main Unit of the prison. It's been closed for a few years. Instead of tearing down the long brick dormitory style buildings that stand side by side, their too small windows evenly spaced and covered with metal mesh, it has been left standing on purpose. The movie companies rent it by the day. From the outside it doesn't look like they changed anything. The buildings are still surrounded by two fences only a few feet apart topped with curls of barbed wire. The dirt patch at the end of the buildings still has basketball hoops, minus the webbing. And no benches. The last time I was inside it, a few years ago, it was still a prison.

I drive past the housing building everyone calls the "murph." It took a year or so of doing criminal defense before I figured out what that meant. All I knew was that all my clients that were going to prison wanted to be housed there, and anyone who was already in prison wanted to be transferred there. I could tell the "murph" was the place to be, but I still couldn't figure out the name.

"Can you get me placed in the murph?" They would ask hopefully before sentencing.

"Sorry" I would shake my head no, "where you're placed is up to the Department of Corrections, not the judge."

Most of my clients are in the county jail, the temporary holding place for people waiting for trial. Once convicted, they move up to the prison system. If you're already in prison, and then commit a new crime, and the District Attorney wants to make your life even more miserable than it already is, instead of punishing you by taking away some of your good time or putting you in segregation, they charge you with the new crime. You get a lawyer, go to trial, and then, if you're convicted, you don't start serving your new sentence until you've finished your old one. The prisoner I am going to see is charged with trying to bring drugs into the prison. They say a guard was paid to smuggle it in to him, or some other inmate, who was going to give it to him. My client's involvement is something like talking with other inmates about whose family members on the outside were going to pay the guard to make it happen. He is currently serving a life sentence. If he's convicted of the drug crime, he will start serving that sentence once he's dead.

The first time I had to drive to the prison to meet with a client, like I am doing now, I passed by a housing unit that had a dark wooden sign with lettering neatly etched in it and painted white: Minimum Restrict Facility. Oh I get it, M.R.F. Murph.

I park in the long lot outside of the maximum security building and bring only four things with me: my file with the few pages of police reports clipped to it, a pen, and my driver's license and Bar card, still out on the passenger seat. I will turn in my keys and ID cards to the guard at the entrance to the building and get a visitor badge in exchange.

I have given the guard my identification and keys and he waves me on to the metal detector. My shoes set it off, as usual. I am wearing low heels and a plain, unflattering gray skirt and gray smock top with a big white collar. It's unflattering because it's maternity. I'm wearing it because I'm six months pregnant. I hold my arms out to my sides and the guard passes the wand around the outline of my body. It only goes off at my shoes. He flips through my file and tells me I'm cleared to go in.

Once when I was at a medium security prison to interview a witness, the guard unscrewed the back of my little tape recorder and looked inside. That was after I got in trouble with the guard at the gate for having a weapon in my car. An expandable steel coil baton. I said I didn't know I couldn't bring it, was planning to leave it in my car, and begged to be let in. I had driven three hours to get there. He locked my baton in one of the little metal boxes reserved for police officer's guns. I got a laminated index card with a number on it in the trade. If weapons don't come inside the gates then prisoners can't get any weapons. He let me in, but I had to apologize and promise I would never again bring a weapon with me when coming to a prison.

Having been cleared and carrying my file and pen, I wait in the lobby until another guard comes to escort me down a winding staircase to the attorney visiting room. The lobby looks like any other government building. Clean white linoleum floors, cinder block walls painted light blue, a chunky white water fountain coming out of the wall, and closed office doors with name plates on them. But there are two differences: the smell, which is somewhere between a hospital and the back of the vet's office where the anxious animals wait in kennels; and the company, which is non-existent. I am alone, but for the guard who let me in.

Eventually my escort comes. He knows who I am here to see since I had to make my appointment in advance. He calls a bunch of numbers and letters on the radio clipped on his shoulder and a loud clunk comes from the door in front of us; the heavy lock responding to the button that the guard on the other end of the radio pushed. He opens the door to the cement stairway and we snake down it, my heels echoing loudly off the steps and walls. I hear the door clunk again behind us. It has not only closed, but locked. At the bottom of the stairs will be another heavy locked door. We will wait behind it, awkwardly smiling at each other, like strangers in an elevator, until it is unlocked by the unseen guard in the control room and we start walking again. The heavy clunk of the lock will echo behind us. We are in the basement, I think. The stairway was long enough that I think we have descended about two floors. There aren't any windows, but that doesn't necessarily mean we are below ground. We walk down a skinny hallway and the officer calls for one more door to open. He holds the door open for me but doesn't enter himself. This is the room where I will meet with my client.

I squeeze myself into this small room with what looks like a mini ping pong table taking up much of the space. There is a chair on each side of the table, and nothing else. There is a six inch wooden barrier rising up from the middle of the wooden table dividing it neatly in half, my court and my client's court. This is supposed to keep us from touching or passing anything back and forth. Another guard sits watching us from the window of a raised office, looking down through the plexiglass wall in front of him like the referee. Our conversation is confidential so the guard is not supposed to listen, only watch. I guess if my client comes over the divider and attacks me, the guard will call someone who will eventually make his way through all of the locked doors between him and me and come to my rescue. Of the hundreds of times I have been locked in rooms with my criminal clients over the years, this has never happened.

The only rule I have to follow is that I can't touch my client. They don't even trust the lawyers not to pass the prisoner a paperclip or packet of cocaine. There will be no introductory handshake.

My client is a middle aged Hispanic man, graying black hair, and a little heavy from the prison food and near complete lack of exercise. He wears the standard plain green pants and short sleeved shirt. He looks about sixty, but I know from the police reports that he is in his forties. I stand when he is brought into the room, smile, and say hello. He looks me over but doesn't say anything. Prison policy is that he not be told in advance that I am coming to see him. He also won't know when he is going to court. This is supposed to minimize the chance of him arranging for an escape or contraband exchange. He doesn't know who I am or why he has been brought to see me.

"I'm Sheri. I'm the lawyer representing you on your new charges." He just looks at me as we both sit down. Silence.

"You a public defender?"

I know that the right answer is no. Anything free must suck.

"No. I'm a private attorney. I have an office in Espanola. The public defender has hired me to represent you because there are so many defendants in your case. Each one needs his own lawyer and they ran out." More silence. I continue with my now automatic introductory speech. "My job is to help you. Anything you tell me is confidential. I won't tell anyone else what you say without your permission. Not the police, not the prosecutor, and not the judge (for juveniles I add 'and not your parents'). The best way I can help you is if you tell me the truth." He nods, still not sure he should trust me.

I know what he needs to hear before he'll let down his guard. He thinks that the State is paying me, which is true, and the State is prosecuting him, which is also true, so I must actually be working with the prosecutor, which is not true.

"Usually people *hire* me to represent them. They pay me. A lot. For a case like this I would usually charge about ten thousand dollars. But you don't have to pay anything. The public defender has to pay my bill." A faint smile. I don't tell him that they will pay me a fixed rate of six hundred dollars.

"You don't work for the State?"

"No. I work for you." He considers this for a moment and then he nods and loosens up his tight mouth.

"So. Do you want to talk about this case?" I look up at the guard behind the Plexiglas and reassure my client, "He can't hear us."

My client tilts his head and raises an eyebrow.

"At least that's what they tell me" and I roll my eyes, like we both know it isn't true.

I'm uncomfortable with the silence so I start talking. I tell him that I see he is doing life, and that any sentence he would get for this new case would be served after his current sentence, and we both know that won't really matter, and that if he wants a trial I would be happy to do it for him, and that it would at least be a break from his usual routine, twenty-three hours a day lock down, he would have at least two court appearances leading up to the trial, and then a day in court for jury selection, and then one or two days more in the actual trial. I would bring you lunch on the trial days. At least I would try. They usually let me, but I can't guarantee it.

More silence.

"Bert's Burger Bowl is near the courthouse. I usually go there. They have good green chili cheeseburgers. The fries are no good though." I pause. "But they're probably better than what you get here."

He laughs a little. One meal from a real restaurant would probably make all of this worth it.

"Do you want me to go over the charges and the possible penalties?"

"No."

"Do you want me to read the police reports to you?"

"No."

"If you want to have a trial I would interview all the witnesses that work at the prison in order to prepare. Whatever guards are going to testify against you. It might screw up an afternoon for them. Make them a little uncomfortable to have to answer my questions." A way to give my client a little power over the guards, even if only by proxy, and then only for a few hours.

"No. They're all right."

Silence.

"My job is to do what you want. What do you want me to do?"

He considers this for a moment. "I just want this over with. Get me a plea."

"Okay."

"And I can read."

"What?" He just looks at me. "Oh." I say after a few second pause. "I know you can read" I lie, since I'm never sure, "but I can't pass you the police reports to read yourself so that's why I said I would read them to you. Of course you can read."

More silence

"I like math. I like to read books about math. Like school books. What do you call em'?" A pause. He is talking slowly by choice. No reason to rush. "Textbooks. They have some in the library. With math, everything has an answer."

I put down my pen, sit back and rest my hands on my lap, letting him know I will stay and listen for as long as he wants to talk. "I stink at math, but I know what you mean."

He lived just outside of Espanola. He knows right where my office is. Near the post office. He has kids, but they don't come visit. Something that has to do with what their mother told them. Did I go to school in Espanola? What do they grow in Connecticut, same as here? How could I leave my family? Don't they miss me? My husband's family isn't here either? Utah! Is he one of those what-do-ya'-call-its with all the wives? I hope not, I say. We laugh. A plea hearing is quick. You won't have to stay through lunch like with a trial. I won't be able to bring you anything to eat.

After about half an hour I have to use the bathroom. Usually how it is these days. I tell him so. I wave to the referee in the box and I see him talk into his radio. The door opens to the little room and my client is told to get up to go. I stay in the room knowing that we leave separately. The guard can't be in charge of both of us at once. My client has been handcuffed the whole time. I tell him I will get back to him with a plea and that it was nice to meet him. He smiles and nods and the guard points him down the hallway in the opposite direction that I came from. In a few minutes a different guard comes to escort me out. Back in the lobby, alone again, I use the bathroom. Every prison I have ever been in has been clean. Inmate labor.

I am seven months pregnant by the time the plea hearing comes around. Another inmate involved in the same crime is entering a plea today as well. I am at the defense table with another attorney. We wait for our clients to be brought in. Their hands are cuffed together, and then to the chain that goes around their waists. Their ankles have handcuffs around them connected with a short chain so they have to take unnaturally small steps. The prosecutor doesn't look up from his paperwork when the two of them clink in, four guards surrounding them. The court reporter is checking the recording equipment and the bailiff is sitting in the witness stand, looking bored. I tell the guard that my client will have to sign papers. The other lawyer says the same. The guards unhook the handcuffs from the waist chain and then from each other.

I welcome my client to sit next to me at the table. I quickly go through the papers with him that he needs to sign before we start the hearing, knowing the judge could walk in at any minute.

"I need to tell you the rights you have that you give up when you enter a plea" I don't need to look at the Guilty Plea Proceeding form in front of me. I have memorized it by repeating it so many times. I can even recite it in Spanish. For my client's benefit I run my finger under the lines as I say them:

You have the right to a trial by jury.

You have the right to the assistance of counsel at all stages of the proceedings. An attorney will be appointed to you free of charge if you can't afford one.

At a trial the State must present all of the evidence and witnesses they have against you and you have the right to cross examine their witnesses as to their truthfulness.

You have the right to compel witnesses to appear on your own behalf and to testify.

You have the right to present evidence on your own behalf.

You have the right to remain silent and be presumed innocent and the burden is on the state to prove that you are guilty beyond a reasonable doubt.

And, the judge needs to know that your plea is voluntary and not the result of force or threats and that no one has promised you anything in exchange for your plea other than what is contained in the written plea agreement.

And finally, *any conviction can have an effect on your immigration status if you are not a US citizen.*

He looks at me hopefully after this last one. "You mean, I could be deported?" We both smile. "The law says I have to tell you."

"All rise!" the bailiff is out of the witness chair looking official. The judge climbs the three stairs to the bench and sits looking down at us. Then we sit.

"Appearances" he calls to us.

"(loud male voice saying a name)…for the State."

The lawyer next to me stands. "(Other loud male voice saying a name)…for the Defendant, uh, uh, Mister…" he looks through papers and then announces a Hispanic surname.

I stand. "Sheri Raphaelson for…" I gesture to my client sitting next to me and say his name, from memory. This little display of respect takes about fifteen seconds of effort and it upsets me that the other attorneys don't bother.

We tell the judge about the plea, he asks the defendants a list of questions then… *I find that your pleas are given freely and voluntarily…I find there is a factual basis for the pleas…I find that under the circumstances the pleas are reasonable…you are sentenced to… to be served consecutive to cause number…*

"All rise!" The judge whooshes off the bench, his black robe ballooning out behind him. The court reporter stays seated, pushing the final buttons on the tape machine. The bailiff is leaning over the bench collecting up the judge's papers. The prosecutor is writing on his file. The other defense attorney is shoving his papers into his briefcase that leans against the leg of the table while he mumbles something to his client, who bends over slightly to hear. Two guards move towards my client, one has the handcuffs open.

"I'll send you copies of the paperwork." I reach to shake his hand and then remember what he told me at our meeting: The worst thing about "here," the maximum unit of the state penitentiary, is never being touched.

In prison when the guard comes to take him out of his cell, he backs up to a mail slot in the otherwise solid metal door and puts his hands together behind him. The guard reaches through the slot and slaps on the handcuffs. Once the cuffs click shut, the guard opens the door. This is the same slot that his food tray is placed on. He's not allowed to reach for it until the hand that placed it there is gone. Since he's in maximum security his time in the yard, a fenced in area no bigger than a child's bedroom, is spent alone. Sometimes it's sunny. He likes feeling the sun warm his skin. Close to a touch, but not quite the same.

They don't even do pat down searches anymore like when he first went in. There's a new metal detector *chair*, the B.O.S.S. chair (The B is for 'body', the O for 'orifice' and one of the S's is 'search', I think). The B.O.S.S. chair has improved staff safety by eliminating the need for any actual physical contact with the inmate when he returns from court or the visiting room.

The few times he's been really sick have actually been okay. There's a bathtub in the infirmary. He used to love taking baths. He would do some of his best thinking alone in a hot bath. His most depressing thought of all isn't that he'll never be able to eat a fresh tomato from his garden, or go to his mother's funeral, or let his hand bump against the wind out the driver's side window, or decide when the light over his bed is turned on or off. That's sad, but he's gotten over it. The thought that provokes the most regret is that he may never take a bath again.

The hearing now over, my professional relationship with him is over as well. I will never see him again. As I'm shaking his hand I decide to be generous with my freedoms and put my left arm around his back and give him a quick half hug. It's not much, but why not.

"Take care" I tell him, smiling. "It's been nice to get to know you." And I mean it. I feel guilty that I can take a bath when I get home, but I won't. It wastes too much time.

I look at the table and pretend to organize my papers when the guards clink and clang all the locks and hooks that are hanging off of the chain around his waist. I don't want to watch. It seems so unnecessary, like when the vet automatically put a muzzle on my dog just because he was a Rottweiler.

"Just be nice to him and he won't bite you." I pleaded with the vet. "He's really quite gentle."

"You never know with this kind." He said, shaking his head from side to side.

After that appointment I switched vets.

One guard stands on each side of my client. His hands are cuffed tightly to each other and hooked onto the loops of chain going around his waist. This way he can't move his hands away from his body. The guards each grab onto one side of the waist chain and walk him out of the courtroom. They have to walk slowly since he can only shuffle because of the short chain between his ankles. The guards will walk him past the other courtrooms to the holding cell. The people waiting nervously for their cases to be called will back up against the wall, startled and momentarily distracted from their own worries, and let the prisoner and the guards pass. More modern courthouses have private hallways just for inmates. As I hear my client's clanking grow more distant I finish writing the summary of the hearing on the front of his file, and the final note for my secretary, 'TO BE CLOSED.' I am done.

Many police reports, jail visits, search warrant inventory lists, "Sheri Raphaelson for..." court appearances, and phone calls with worried mothers and girlfriends later, I get the letter. My secretary is out to lunch when the mail comes and I'm looking at the sealed envelope. It's one of the preprinted envelopes from the penitentiary that inmates are required to use for outgoing mail. I stare for a moment at the name written on the return address line, followed by the required five digit inmate number. It has been a few months and I don't remember him immediately, but then it comes to me. I'm holding the still sealed envelope and trying to figure out what's inside. I can't imagine why he's writing to me. His case is over. Did my secretary forget to send the copies of the signed plea paperwork? My first thought is always that I've done something wrong.

I leave the rest of the mail on my secretary's desk but take the letter back to my office and open it. It's written in the kind of perfect script that only an elementary school teacher, or lots of time, can produce.

"Thank you for the paperwork and all your help." He got the paperwork so why is it such a long letter? What did I forget to do?

The next paragraph is spent trying to list all the synonyms for "awe." There is "shock," "amazement," "unexpected gift," and more. It's clear he's not asking me to do anything. Not telling me what I've done wrong. This is odd. It doesn't feel like I should be reading it under the fluorescent lights of my office, with the door wide open.

I go on reading. There is a long section devoted to wondering about all of the possible motivations for kind actions. And then there is something about me being brave. And "in front of the guards." And then "in front of the other lawyers." In front of "the people you work with everyday."

And prayers and good wishes for the new life growing inside of me that, with all due respect, will surely be as beautiful as I am.

And then about him. How he couldn't move from the surprise of it all. How he doesn't even remember walking back to the holding cell down the hall. It was like he was in a hot air balloon and was floating. No handcuffs, no chains, no green uniform, no guards. Not even noticing all the people in the halls staring at him and moving away.

And how good it made him feel inside. Not like that. Don't misunderstand. Not that at all. But just a human thing. Feeling like *he* was human.

How his faith in the Lord has been renewed because only Jesus could be responsible for sending him an Angel. Me. I'm the Angel. (I'm the Angel?)

I'm about to cry. This isn't what I expected. I'm at work. I have stacks of very formal stationery with my name and the words 'attorney at law' printed on it in raised black lettering. I'm wearing lipstick and eyeliner.

He writes that he was caught off guard. So am I. I too am surprised and amazed. I am suddenly overwhelmed by the ability of this letter to interrupt my life as an endless robotic to-do list, and elevate it to something that makes the stacks of papers in my office disappear. I too am floating down the hallway and not noticing the people around me.

I'm not reading a letter that was written in a smelly, concrete cell, full with the same nothing every day, but instead I'm reading the rainbow colored lines that reflect on the wall when I sit near a window and accidentally hold my watch at just the right angle. I'm reading the thoughts in someone's mind that are so new they aren't organized into words yet but are just buzzing fire flies between brain cells. I'm reading the uncomfortable feeling you share with the stranger in the dressing room who forgot to lock the door you just opened. I'm reading a letter that is more beautiful than what follows the words "how do I love thee, let me count the ways" and more painful than being six and told that your cat has gone up into the sky to be with all the other cats so she can play and be happy for ever and ever.

I am reading the last line of a letter that starts very formally "Dear Attorney Raphaelson" and then flows like water rushing down a mountain. I have read the letter like I was following the water, running next to the stream, becoming more and more curious to find out where the water will lead to. I have run next to the stream all the way to the end; to the place where it flattens out and runs into a fast moving river.

I am at the end of his letter. I am about to find out what exactly he thinks I did that made his piece of earth turn just a little faster, made gravity pull him just a little bit stronger. I will learn what I did that somehow wiggled a magic wand and changed his pale isolation into a colorful beach towel.

This single line is the final paragraph. "You touched me, just like I was a regular person. Thank you."

6

When Was the Last Time You Felt the Baby Move?

I had never delivered a dead baby before. I had been a midwife for three years and had never even seen the delivery of a stillborn. The closest I came was when I was a student in training. One of the clinic patients came in saying she wanted to be examined. She didn't have an appointment, the afternoon was booked solid, and although she was full term, she said she wasn't in labor. The student midwife tried to send her home, explaining the signs of labor and telling her to come back when it's time. The mother wouldn't leave. She was very polite, insisted that everything was fine, but wouldn't leave until someone examined her.

The midwife relented, took her to an examination room and began with the standard questions for someone at the end of the pregnancy. No she wasn't having contractions. No she wasn't bleeding. No her water hadn't broken. No she wasn't feeling faint or having bad headaches. And yes, the baby has been moving normally. The student midwife listened for the heart and heard nothing. She ran her hands over the stretched belly, tracing the outline of the baby one more time to make sure she was listening over the heart. She was. Still nothing. She called in the staff midwife. The same.

A healthy baby twisted up in the cord. A placenta that stops pumping blood. Or the most common reason, which is also the hardest one for the mother to accept: who knows. That doesn't go very far in answering the question the mother will ask, at first out loud and then in later years only to herself: why?

When a baby has died inside it is helpful to the midwife to know how long it has been dead. One way to determine this is to find out from the mother when the movement stopped. It's nicer to ask the question in the positive: when was the last time you felt the baby move? The student midwife asked this question to the mother who had come in wanting to be examined. She was now on the examining table, having been told that a beating heart could not be heard. The answer wasn't very helpful; "I feel the baby moving right now." I wanted to cry and I wasn't even there. I was hearing the story the next day, in class. This mother obviously needed a little more time to believe what she must have already suspected when she came into the clinic maintaining that everything was fine. Fortunately there's no real rush to get the baby out.

She was sent to the hospital, an ultrasound was done to confirm the baby was dead, and then the doctor started her labor artificially. It will almost always start on its own, eventually, but doctors usually choose to get it going right away. Each way has its emotional benefits to the mother and I don't know which is better. Benefits to the baby are no longer a consideration. I have never had a baby die in my own practice. Early miscarriages-yes. Full grown viable babies-no.

This was why I had come to this busy hospital in Jamaica. To help, but mostly to learn. To be involved in deliveries that in my own practice I would pass on to a doctor, the law deciding they were too complicated for a midwife. The delivery I was about to do would be my first stillborn.

By the time the mother I was to deliver was on the bed in the delivery room it had already been determined that the baby was dead. I don't know how. The paperwork, if there was any, didn't come with the mother into the delivery room. Knowing any medical history of the woman, besides her immediate condition; she's ready to push out a baby, didn't seem to matter. I had surmised that anything else was more like unnecessary gossip. I was only there for a week and I was trying very hard to politely integrate into the system they already had, not change, question, or criticize it.

I might have heard someone say a rural clinic sent the mother to the big hospital where I was working after the nurse there determined the baby was dead. I wasn't really sure. Maybe she was in the city all along and stopped feeling movement so she came in on her own. All I was focusing on was the present moment and the minutes to come. The very experienced midwife who was assigning midwives to patients asked if I had ever delivered a stillborn. When I said no, which was the truth, I thought this would disqualify me for doing the delivery. I was wrong. She pointed me to the bed. Here was a hugely pregnant woman, in labor, and I was going to deliver her dead baby.

The woman was silently pushing in the heavy humidity of the summer. The only air conditioning in the large third floor delivery room was a bank of windows open wide letting a nearly undetectable breeze invisibly ruffle the air over the six beds that lined the walls. Most of the other Americans in Jamaica that week, tourists at the resort beaches, were no doubt complaining about the heat as they lay under a shade umbrella sipping a cold drink, able to sneak back to their air conditioned rooms when they wanted a break.

The sink in the delivery room had cold water only that came out in a thin trickle. There was one dried up piece of soap nearby. Between deliveries we all tried to tease some bubbles out of it as we did our best to wash our hands. A few days later the soap was gone.

The pushing mother's face was wet with sweat, but not tears. Crying wouldn't make it any easier. I put on gloves and stood by her side next to her bent knee. She would push with the contractions and then relax in between. Usually the Jamaican midwives directed the women to push continuously and scolded those who took breaks. No matter how hard a woman was pushing they would tell her to push harder. It seemed harsh, but with no fetal heart monitors and no sophisticated emergency services it made some sort of sense to hurry the birth once it was imminent. There was no helping a sick baby until it was out.

No one told this woman to rush. The midwife who chose me for the delivery was right next to me, and two others standing near by. Everyone was uncharacteristically still, the mother determining the speed of things. The metronome was swinging very slowly for this song. When the baby's head was visible I put my hands near it, but knew it would take a few more pushes for it to actually come out. I was wrong. With that one push not just the head but the whole baby practically flew out. I jerked my hands closer and barely caught it before it dropped onto the bed. I was embarrassed that I almost missed it.

"These one's come fast," the midwife next to me murmured. "No resistance." I felt a little better about having been surprised. I laid the baby on the bed between the mother's legs and cut the cord. Everything seemed so quiet and slow, not like a birth usually is:

A rush to examine the baby.

Look for a breath.

Dry the baby and keep it warm.

The mother craning to see.

A relief of happiness.

Getting the baby and mother back together as soon as possible.

Lots of action.

This was like no kind of birth I had ever attended. The other midwife would insightfully remark later that the name 'stillbirth' describes not only the condition of the baby, but the stillness in the delivery room as well.

The other midwife nodded that she would deliver the placenta and I carried the baby to the little table where antibiotic drops are normally put in the eyes and a shot of Vitamin K injected into the tiny thigh. This baby looked perfect. Chubby. Sleeping.

As a midwife in the United States I can't officially declare a death, however here, where there aren't nearly enough doctors to go around, it would be offensive to bother a doctor for something this obvious. I learned in EMT school that you have to listen for the heart for one full minute before you can determine someone is dead. I put my stethoscope on the chest. As the minute progressed my eyes got wetter. I kept thinking I was seeing the chest rise with little breaths. There was complete silence in my ears. The baby was big, probably around seven pounds. I can't remember if I weighted it, but I imagine I did.

The minute was up. I wrapped the baby in a blanket. It didn't need to be kept warm, but new babies get wrapped in blankets. The mother hadn't delivered the placenta yet. The other midwife was poking at her belly trying to encourage it to come.

I carried the baby back to the mother. I stood by her side, this time at her shoulder, not her knee. I didn't ask if she wanted to hold it, I just handed her the bundle. She looked at the little face in silence. Whose round face? Whose arched eyebrows? She pulled back the blanket and looked at the hands and feet, no doubt counting the ten fingers and toes.

"You grew a perfect baby" I spoke carefully knowing that my words may become a permanent part of her memory "you did everything right."

The midwife was massaging her belly trying to stimulate more contractions. Only part of her placenta had let go, the rest firmly adhered to the inside of her uterus. Blood was leaking out from behind the spot that had come loose. The entire placenta would have to come out before her uterus could squeeze into a tight ball and stop the bleeding. The squeezing of more contractions would help push the rest of the placenta out. Until then, the mother would continue to lose blood.

Not until the placenta is out is the birth completely over. She wasn't having any more contractions so the placenta wasn't budging. If I was that mother, I would hold onto the placenta too, not wanting the birth to be over. Hoping that somehow it could still have a different ending.

The blood loss wasn't much. Yet. But if it kept up it would be a problem. The midwife had just injected the mother with pitocin to cause contractions. Still nothing. If she kept bleeding, and the pitocin didn't start to work soon to push that placenta off, the midwife would have to put her whole hand inside the mother's vagina and then further through her still open cervix and into her uterus, only her elbow visible. Then she would peel the placenta off with her fingers. Even in the United States, with pain medication for the mother, this is still terribly painful. Worse than the birth.

When you are about to do this your assistant moves to the head of the bed and puts her hands on the mother's shoulders. This is not the act of caring that it seems to the mother. This is to hold her down when she tries to squirm up the bed, away from the hand inside her. Not only is it painful, but it also dramatically increases the mother's chance of getting an infection inside her uterus. It is worth avoiding unless the blood loss is so severe that there is no choice.

The other midwife was at the end of the bed still poking at the mother's belly trying to either start some contractions or keep some weak ones from stopping. She looked worried. I was only vaguely aware of this happening. I was looking at the mother look at her baby, trying to figure out when she was done. Would it be in a minute or an hour? Just as I wondered how much longer the efficient Jamaican midwives would allow her to keep the baby, one had already shot me a look when I handed the baby to the mother, probably dreading how long it would take to get it back, the mother tucked the blanket gently back around the baby and gave me a nod. She was ready. I reached down and the mother pulled the baby back just a little. Maybe she wasn't ready. She looked up to the ceiling and spoke softly.

"Thank you Jesus for sparing *my* life."

Now she was done. She easily handed the baby to me. I stood there just behind her head and realized I didn't know what to do. I figured I was supposed to bring the baby somewhere, but I had no idea where that might be. If the mother was done I knew I shouldn't still have the baby in the room. No one was telling me anything. The one midwife who was waiting on the placenta was giving the mother another shot in her thigh. The other midwives were off doing other things in the large delivery room, probably deliveries, their backs to me.

I walked out into the hall pretending I knew where I was going. I stood on the other side of the door, holding that baby tight to my chest, and I cried. I cried all the tears that the mother had inside but couldn't release, just like her placenta, because then it would really be over. I cried all the tears the baby would have cried in this lifetime but held in for the next. Even after one of the midwives came into the hall and took the baby from me, disappearing into a long closet like room that I was sure not to go into the remainder of my stay, I kept crying. No noise, just tears.

I've delivered plenty of babies that weren't breathing, and a few whose hearts weren't beating. I get them breathing, get the hearts started, or both. Rub, blow, press, cajole, promise, curse, or whatever that particular baby needs. But those babies have never seemed dead to me, they just haven't started yet. There's a difference somehow. The baby that is going to start is full of - something, the baby that isn't, is, well, empty.

Later I would have a mother in my own practice who had decided she was done having children. She had a doctor's appointment to get an IUD, and at the appointment she learned, to her disappointment, she was pregnant.

A lot of our prenatal appointments were spent with her trying to figure out how she was going to deal with taking care of a new baby along with the little ones she already had.

She carried the baby one week past her due date, putting off the reality of this unexpected baby as long as she could. She stoically went through the hours of contractions and was finally ready to push. Out came the head and then, instead of the body, nothing. Half in/half out—what my sisters and I used to shout the instant our station wagon lined up with the signs thanking us for visiting Connecticut (where we lived) and welcoming us to Massachusetts (where my grandmother lived).

This baby was half in/half out, the mother still not ready for it to be here. I had to reach in and move the baby's shoulder in order to get it out from behind the pubic bone where it was tightly wedged, preventing anything past the head from coming out. The doctor who delivered her first baby had cut a large episiotomy. I could see the scar. No doubt he too experienced the body get stuck. Although the solution comes from the inside, and enlarging the opening on the outside doesn't actually help, it is a panic response I can understand.

After thirty seconds of maneuvering this large baby in this tight space, a space made even tighter by having both of my hands occupying it as well as the baby, I got the shoulder loose and the body started to come out. I did what I always do at this point, called to the mother to reach down and finish the delivery.

It is just incredible to see a mother lift her own baby out. What I see from between the mother's legs is what the baby sees; the mother's face. My favorite moment is when the baby is suspended over the mother's belly, legs dangling, teeny back encircled with the mother's large hands, the umbilical cord stretched between both of their legs, and the emotion just pouring out from the mother's smile. Although the mother usually brings the baby close into her chest only seconds later, it is that moment, the in between moment when their faces meet, that stays with me; the baby in the foreground, and the smile in the background. At that moment I know love is a noun because I am looking at it. Of all of the intimate touching and poking that I do during the labor and birth it is at that moment only, when the mother and baby first see each other, when I feel like I am intruding.

"Take your baby, take your baby, reach down, two hands!" With the shoulder no longer stuck behind that bone the body is ready the squirm out. The mother doesn't move. I pull the rest of the baby out myself and put it on her belly. The mother lets her head drop back onto the pillow, her eyes closed. No smile for the love to leak out of. It was an exhausting labor and the mother was just relieved to have it over with. I understood, but the baby didn't. The baby needed to see the smile, to feel the warm hands wrapped around its body, to be hit with a giant piece of flying love, to get the look that says "nice to meet you baby, I'm your mother and this is my face, and now that I've seen you I've gotten a blueprint of your soul etched in a secret spot in my brain and, like a micro-chip in a lost dog, I will always be able to find you and make sure you're taken care of," to be told that it was wanted. The baby needed to be told to stay.

It was a few minutes before the breathing problems started. The color was never quite right, the hands and feet blue long past when they should have been getting pink. I was waiting for the placenta and my assistant was watching the baby. A few times I told her the color didn't look good, to rub the baby to get it to cry and take some deep breaths. Nothing alarming, yet, but the breathing needed to be a little deeper for the baby to get enough oxygen. Then the placenta came. The birth is officially over. If this baby is going to survive it is going to be because the mother chooses to take care of it, wants it to live. We all know that dark feeling of being where we aren't wanted; the party only your friend was invited to but brought you along anyway. If we had our own ride and could leave, we would. For this baby leaving is easy.

First the skin around the lips got blue. Then the breathing got too fast and shallower. Then the stomach sucked in as the baby used the wrong muscles to take a breath. The nostrils flared as the baby struggled to get air.

The oxygen was turned on. 911 called to this little town in the mountains. Yes, someone will wait in the street to direct the ambulance. The hospital is called. The charge nurse tells me they'll be ready and thanks me for calling. The baby is double wrapped for warmth. A stethoscope from my ears to its chest as I count the breaths and look at my watch. I'm mentally ready for the heart to slow and I whisper to my assistant three—to—one, reminding her of the ratio of compressions to breaths in anticipation of us starting CPR.

The mother gets worried. She starts talking to the baby. A status call to 911. The ambulance is thirty minutes away. I'm rocking the baby, whispering in its ear, "your momma loves you. Everything's going to be just fine. You stay here sweetie. Your momma wants you here." Then the breathing getting calmer. The breaths deeper. The blue becomes pink. The respiratory rate normal. The oxygen is turned off. Another call to 911. They're only ten minutes away? Well, send them back. Everything's fine. His vitals are normal. The mother is holding the baby and nursing. Yes, I'm sure. My responsibility? Spell my last name? My license number? Yes, I understand perfectly. Really, everything is all right. Yes, I'm certain.

One birth I had the parents had separated during the pregnancy, the mother, bitter, didn't want the father at the birth, but hadn't told him. She was simply not going to call him until after it was over. One day he called, innocently, from work on his lunch break, to see how she was doing. She was in labor. She talked quickly, getting off the phone before the next contraction, me and my assistant quiet, as she requested, in the background. That baby wasn't only born breathless but with a slowing heart rate as well.

As my assistant and I did CPR the mother, a doctor herself, was looking on with worry, telling the baby how much she loved it. The baby would struggle to take a few breaths but then stop, the heart rate flattening along with the chest. I knew that mechanically we could keep the heart and lungs going from the outside with CPR, but that it would take something more for the baby to start those things from the inside. Then something told me to say these words: 'your daddy loves you.' They came into my thoughts with some urgency and I blurted them out, not even thinking about how it would sound to the mother. I was still doing CPR. Almost immediately the breathing improved. I said it again: 'your daddy loves you.' Within a minute the baby was breathing on its own, CPR no longer necessary and the baby being helped only by a little extra oxygen blowing under its nose, the heart rate steadily climbing to normal.

When my son was seven he asked me if I ever delivered a baby who died. I told him the story of the brave mother in Jamaica. A baby who did have a mother who was ready to give it all of the love it needed, but who died anyway. I was afraid my son would be upset. He was silent for a while and then asked two questions; was the baby a boy or a girl, and, were the eyes open.

I remember my heart sinking when the midwife pointed me to the bed to do the delivery, I remember the stillness, I remember the baby popping out all at once, I remember looking at my watch for that long quiet minute, I remember the mother's soft voice as she thanked Jesus, I remember crying outside the door and later hiding in the bathroom to cry some more, I remember the midwife coming out of the long hallway with empty arms. I remember realizing that the mothers are too poor to pay for funerals and the hospital disposes of the stillborns. Incinerated with the other medical waste. But to my son's questions, both of which seem like obvious things for someone to wonder about under the circumstances, the answers were the same: I don't know.

Since that time I have tried to figure out why I noticed certain things, and why I didn't notice others. The whole experience was given to me because, I believe, it will help me to help someone else in the future. I don't think it was an accident that *I* delivered that dead baby. I gave the baby to the mother to hold when the Jamaican midwives wouldn't have. Holding the baby in the hall, crying over it, and then crying without it, needed to happen to keep a certain balance in the world. Maybe a certain number of tears need to be shed for each death. It doesn't matter whose eyes they come from, but the total number of freed tears must be equal, in a certain proportion, to all the deaths that day. That week, that year, that century, or however frequently God, or whomever, balances the ledger.

The numerous variations I have seen in the way that one solitary event occurs, giving birth, has made me stop trying to figure out why, but has led me to believe that it is all for a reason that I will never understand. That I don't need to understand, I just need to let happen.

"How long will my labor take?"

"How ever long it needs to." How ever long you need to accept that you are going to be a mother. How ever long it takes you to get to the point where you are sure you can't do it for even another minute, but then you do, and later you use that memory to remind yourself of all the other seemingly impossible things you can and will get through. How ever long it takes for the baby to be convinced that someone on the outside is ready to take care of it. How ever long it takes for the friend who is with you during the labor to casually ask the midwife the one question that occurred to her for no reason she can figure out, the answer to which she will use years later to save a life.

Do the babies always cry?

No, sometimes you have to kind of aggravate them to get them to start breathing.

Aggravate them?

Yeah, like I'll rub my hand up and down their back, or poke at the bottom of the foot with something pointy, like the end of a pen.

I don't know why I didn't notice that dead baby's sex, but I did notice that it didn't have much hair, and what it did have was curly and pressed flat on its head. Even though I don't know the reason for remembering that detail, I know there was one, and I'm sure it will someday become important.

7

Cough It Up Baby!

I am standing next to the bed at the far end of the large delivery room, the wall of windows behind me all open. Hot sticky air heavy with Jamaica's ever present humidity is slowly drifting by. I am holding a new baby in my hands just a few inches above the mother's belly, still tethered by the cord coming from between the mother's open legs. We are all wet and sticky; the mother and I from sweat, the baby from amniotic fluid. I instinctively rub the baby's back when it doesn't cry spontaneously. This usually aggravates the baby just enough to make it cry a bit, taking in a deep breath in the process. No cry. No deep breath. I rub a little harder. No shallow breath. I hear only a slight gurgle that I recognize as air trying to pass through thick mucous in the back of the baby's throat.

Normally I would take the blue bulb syringe I bring to every birth and put it far back in the baby's throat and suck out the mucous. Once the obstruction is out of the way, the baby starts breathing. I usually give the bulb syringe to the mother to use over the next few months. It will be handy for her to have when she needs to clean out the baby's stuffy nose. It costs only $1.25. I could clean it and sterilize it, but it's so cheap it isn't worth it. I'll bring a new one to the next birth. In three seconds the struggling baby I am holding could breathe freely with a quick squeeze of a bulb syringe.

But I don't have my usual birth supplies because I'm in a public hospital in Jamaica instead of a comfortable home in the United States. The people are poor. The hospital is poor. The availability of supplies is poor. They don't have bulb syringes. They don't have private rooms. They don't have electronic fetal monitors. They don't even have gowns. The woman is told ahead of time to bring with her a nightgown, a sheet for the delivery bed, and a towel for the midwife to use to dry the baby. What this hospital does have is a very busy delivery room run exclusively by highly skilled midwives. A doctor is a rare sight on the maternity floor, and as far as I can tell, fairly unnecessary. Jamaican music comes from a small radio propped up on the window sill.

There are five beds in this large hot room, each separated by a curtain that is never pulled closed. It is not uncommon for all of the beds to be filled with pushing women and a few midwives keeping track of all of them. Finish one delivery and move on to the next. Maybe washing your hands with the cold water slowly sputtering out of the sink and the end of the bar of soap that might have just one last wash in it. There are no family members or friends. This is all business with no time for thorough explanations preceding every shot or exam, and no room for a busy midwife to step around crowds of well wishers. Fathers wait at home.

Even though there are no bulb syringes, there is one electric suction machine. An older model, but it works. A small electric pump the size of a shoe box with a tip for a disposable plastic tube to attach over. You turn the machine on, put the tube down the baby's throat, and it sucks whatever is in there out through the tube. The tube is long so not only can it reach into the back of the mouth like a bulb syringe, but also deeper into the throat. Electric suction is standard in delivery rooms in the United

States, available next to every bed. This machine will quickly take care of the mucous in the back of my baby's throat.

Across the room a midwife is standing near the suction machine, cleaning up from having just used it. The machine is on a small wooden table. Next to it is a plastic bassinet on a wheeled stand that new babies in U.S. hospitals are wheeled around in. The once see through sides of this one are scratched and dulled from use. The wheels have been removed. In place of a mattress there are folded blankets lining the bottom. This is actually better. A hard surface under the baby makes chest compressions more effective. The baby's heart absorbs the pushing, not the mattress. The one green cylinder of oxygen that is moved around the room as necessary stands in the corner nearby. There is one infant sized oxygen mask made to fit over a full term baby's mouth and nose. I have already watched another midwife squish it to make it fit over a preemie's face. I was pressing on the tiny chest -one and two and three-, and then she would fight to seal the mask over the face with one hand while she squeezed the bag of oxygen with the other, trying to force oxygen into the baby instead of out the sides of the mask. One and two and three and squeeze, one and two and three and squeeze. This area serves as the resuscitation station.

"Can you set up the suction machine please?" I politely call to the midwife as I clamp and cut the cord, freeing the baby for the walk across the room in my arms. The few seconds it would save by having the other midwife get the new tube out of the package and hook it on the machine would be a few seconds sooner this baby would start breathing. After three minutes without adequate oxygen permanent brain damage begins. This baby has been out less than a minute. I will have the airway cleared and the baby breathing in far less than three minutes. Technically I suppose it's an emergency since the airway is blocked, but it is so easy to fix I hardly think of it that way.

Before I even take the first step towards the resuscitation station the midwife calls back over her shoulder, "Sorry, I just used the last tube" and then, as if placing an exclamation point on the situation, holds the used coil of tubing above the large trash can an arms length away to her and lets it drop among the bloody gloves, used syringes, dirty paper towels, and whatever else has accumulated from the last dozen births.

I am frozen in the moment. Using "the last tube" doesn't mean the last tube from the packages stacked up neatly next to the machine, or that someone will have to run down the hall to a supply closet. It means she has used the last tube that there is. Maybe until tomorrow or the next day. Or the next week. The breathing problem I was going to casually correct like I had done so many times before has suddenly turned into a breathing problem that will kill this baby.

No bulb syringe, no electric suction, and a glob of mucous doing a good job of almost completely plugging the airway. I can still hear some gurgling as the baby tries to breathe through the mucous. There's a little air moving, but far less than enough. The baby's skin is starting to darken from lack of oxygen. A few seconds ago the two minutes I had left to clear the airway felt like plenty of time. If time was money the baby would have been breathing and I would be left with a pocket full of change. Now I'm broke.

The room full of moving bodies, grunting women, crying babies and midwives commanding 'push harder' or 'breathe' or 'open da legs wider *mahn*– like when you were getting' da baby in ' disappears like a backdrop on a movie set being rolled away. There is nothing but bright white silence all around me. My world has become the small triangle formed by the mother on the bed beneath me, the baby in my arms, and me standing over it all. I am the top of the pyramid, minus the third eye of wisdom.

I first saw the mother a few minutes earlier when she dragged herself across the hall from the labor room, climbed up on the empty delivery bed, and started to silently push. I gave a reassuring smile, reached over the side of her leg and caught her baby. Now her eyes shift between me and her baby. She too knows the baby should be breathing. She also knows that whatever the suction machine is, I wanted to use it, and now I can't. We have a quick exchange. She politely asks me to save her baby. I promise her I will. Neither one of us has spoken.

Forget rubbing the back to cause some discomfort, I grab the scissor

I used to cut the cord and start poking the bottom of the baby's foot with the points. I angle the baby so the head is lower than the body, giving gravity a chance to help the mucous drain into the mouth. Still no more than a gurgle. I stare at the baby, moving only when I move it. I have to get the mucous out and I have nothing to use—except me. Think. I can suck it out myself. I can put my lips over the baby's lips, suck the mucous into my mouth, and then spit it out. Perfect plan except that right now this small island has one of the highest rates of HIV in the world. There is no standard prenatal testing and I have to assume that all of the women are infected, as are their babies, and the mucous in this babies' throat. I learned from the Jamaican midwives to stand at the mother's side to do the delivery, instead of between her legs where I could be hit with splashing blood or amniotic fluid.

The baby is still struggling to breathe. It has nearly been three minutes. In every way I am holding this baby's life in my hands. I glance at the mother's face, as still as the baby's. This baby shouldn't die because the world can't spare a dollar and a quarter for a bulb syringe.

Ten seconds. If the baby doesn't get the mucous out by the time I count to ten, I'm sucking it out.

One.

Two.

Three.

Four.

I poke its foot even faster, and probably much harder than I intend to.

Five.

Six.

Seven.

I tilt my arm even more, awkwardly lowering the head far below the level of the feet.

Eight.

I'm bringing the baby to my mouth. And then I hear it. A small muffled cough. I hesitate. I don't want to jinx anything by speaking so

I just think it: that's it sweetie, you can do it. Then a big cough and a glob of mucous appears in the baby's mouth. I wipe it out with my gloved finger. There is a weak cry that gets progressively louder. The mother finally exhales. We both smile.

After ten minutes I have delivered the placenta, checked that the mother's blood pressure is normal, and I am accompanying her on the slow walk down the hall to the post-partum ward, the baby in my arms in case the mother faints. I help her into an empty bed, and hand her the baby. It is the first time I hear her speak. "Thank you."

8

Ventana is *Spanish for Window*

I was the first one to cry. There were two other students and one staff midwife sitting with me, all of us fanned out on the wood floor at the feet of the very pregnant woman in the rocking chair as she told us her secret. A few hours earlier she had come knocking on the door of the clinic in the middle of the night. I was sleeping downstairs on the couch in the waiting room. It was my turn to be the one to answer the door. That meant that when someone knocked in the middle of the night I would shake myself awake, brush the wrinkles out of my clothes as I walked to the front door, peer through the glass window at the woman on the other side, and if she was pregnant, undo the locks and let her in. The birth clinic wasn't in the best El Paso neighborhood.

I would turn the lights on in the quiet exam room, examine her, determine if she was in labor, and either send her home with instructions to do the impossible, be patient, or set her up in a birth room and wake up the student whose turn it was to monitor the labor and do the delivery.

When the knock came on the door this night I woke up immediately, only able to fall asleep half way knowing that I might have to get up at any minute. In college I never had to set my alarm for morning classes. Just worrying about getting up in time would make me wake up throughout the night to look at the clock. I pushed the curtain aside and looked out the window to see a very pregnant woman and a Hispanic man in his early thirties. I recognized the woman from having done prenatal appointment with her in the previous months. I knew she was due any time. This was her third or fourth baby. I couldn't remember exactly.

She didn't know any English, unusual for the women who lived near the border, and she always seemed really excited about her appointments. When I would offer her the earpieces of the fetoscope to hear the baby's heart she always took them and listened. For a long time. I even remembered her name, which surprised me since there was such a volume of women coming through the clinic. It had been coincidence that not only was I working on the days when this woman had her appointments, but her chart would be next on the pile when I would emerge from the exam room having finished one appointment and ready to start the next. I couldn't think of any other clients for whom I had been the midwife so many times during her pregnancy.

I always liked her appointments. She was a little older than the usual client, maybe in her mid thirties, and had a very peaceful way about her. She always smiled and never seemed in a hurry. I would feel especially calm when I would take her blood pressure, measure her growing belly, and stumble with my Spanish to ask her about headaches, constipation, and any pain with urination. So tonight, when I saw her at the door I assumed that she was in labor. I was excited that I would be there when she delivered.

I twisted the locks and held the door open. She and the man came into the hall. By the calm look on the woman's face she must be between contractions. She may not have much time to answer questions before the next one started. Skipping the 'good evenings,' I asked what I always did when someone came in the middle of the night:

"*Tiene dolores?*" Are you having contractions?

She shook her head no.

"*Rompio su fuente?*" Did your water break? Sometimes contractions don't start for a few hours.

Again, no.

She had had babies before so I thought she would know better than to come in the middle of the night just for bloody show, but I asked anyway. "*Tiene desecho con sangre?*"

Quietly she answered. "*Tampoco.*" Not that either.

We all stood quietly. The only reason for a pregnant woman to come to a birth clinic in the middle of the night is because she's ready to have her baby.

I looked at the man. Maybe the mother was having a problem understanding my Spanish. He looked like he was from El Paso, not Mexico. Levi's and Nike's. He would speak English and his Spanish would be much better than mine.

"Is she in labor?"

"I don't know. I don't think so."

"Then why are you here? Something must have happened to make you decide to come." I wasn't upset, just confused.

"Oh no, no, no. You don't understand. I'm not with her. I mean, I'm not her husband or anything. I don't even know her."

He was right. I didn't understand. I didn't say anything but must have had a confused look on my face. He continued to explain.

"I just picked her up and gave her a ride. See, she was walking on the side of the highway and I saw she was pregnant. Really pregnant." He tilted his head down towards the big belly next to him. "I stopped to see if she was okay. It didn't make sense why she'd be walking on the highway alone at night."

I was quickly becoming more awake. Not the kind of awake when someone's alternating between breathing hard and screaming, and trying very hard to convince me that she can't do it and I need to just hurry up and get her baby out for her. Not that kind of adrenaline fueled waking that makes my heart beat fast and my mind click through everything that's going to happen in the next few minutes so I can make sure everything I will be reaching for will be no more than an arms length away. This was the kind of awake that gently warmed the figuring-out parts of my brain, as if by turning up a dimmer switch on a light. These would be slow careful thoughts.

She watched me and the man talking, not understanding any of it but able to guess what he was explaining to me. She had a shy smile and was looking down, only stealing occasional glances as me, like a child worried about getting in trouble.

"She told me the name of this place." He continued. "I knew where it was because my cousin's girlfriend had a baby here. That was about a year ago. Well anyway, where I picked her up..." and he tilted his head towards the mother again, "it was so far from this exit she would have been walking for hours. It's a good thing I stopped. She only had those shoes" and he pointed down to her thin rubber flip flops.

He told me the name of the neighborhood she said she had come from before he saw her. It didn't mean anything to me. I was only in El Paso to learn to be a midwife. My familiarity with the city consisted of the routes between my small apartment, the clinic, and the grocery store with the Laundromat next to it. When I wasn't working at the clinic or sitting through classes, I was mostly sleeping.

He estimated she had been walking for a few hours already. He said he offered her some water he had in the truck, but she said no.

Would I take care of her now? he wanted to know. He didn't want to be rude, but he had to get home. And he was really only giving her a ride anyway. Making sure she got here okay. And since she did, well.

"Yes. Of course I'll take care of her. She's a patient here. I know her. Go ahead and leave. And thank you."

She and I were left standing in the hallway of the dark clinic. She had nothing with her but a small purse. She wore a loose cotton dress over her large belly. A *bata*, I had heard it called. It was a warm night. She had long dark hair loosely pulled back. She wasn't in labor, but maybe she thought something was wrong with the baby. I would ask her more questions and then do an exam. I walked a few steps to the filing cabinet to get her chart.

"Lupe Valdez *verdad?*" You're Lupe Valdez, right? I wasn't really asking since I knew that was her name, but I wanted her to know that of all the women who come through the busy clinic, I remembered her.

"*No.*"

I had the file drawer pulled open and was fingering through the "V" charts for hers. I stopped.

"*No?*" I was tired but I was sure that was her name. I looked at her.

She began fumbling for words alternating between saying in Spanish 'yes I am,' 'no that's not me,' 'yes those are my papers,' and 'no that's not my name.' I was completely confused. Then, after a long pause and staring directly into my eyes, she let out a long sigh and began to explain.

The chart that says Lupe Valdez is mine, but that is not my name.

I had the chart in my hand. That was the moment I knew something unusual was unfolding. Something secret. Something special. Something important. I knew that she wouldn't be having a baby that night but I wouldn't be going back to sleep either, and she wouldn't be leaving. She hadn't come to the clinic in the middle of the night after walking for hours and ready to walk for hours more because she needed to be examined. She came for something else.

We looked at each other in silence. The clinic was dark except for the round hall light above her. This was an old two story house that had been converted into a birth clinic. We were standing in the front hall. The light shone straight down, hitting her head and then spreading out in a bright circle. I was in the dim filing cabinet hall, a few feet away from her, waiting for 'it.'

She looked straight at me. "*Mi nombre es Celia Carrillo.*" My name is Celia Carrillo.

Her head dropped into her hands and she began to cry. She kept repeating she was sorry. That we were all so nice. That she didn't want to lie. That she felt terrible about the lying. She didn't think she had a choice. She wanted to tell us but she was afraid. Again, how sorry she was and how nice we were.

"*Esta bien.*" It's alright. "*Aqui, Usted tiene amigas.*" Here, you have friends.

I led her into a vacant birth room. A large bed in the middle with a colorful comforter and lots of pillows and nightstands to each side. Across from the door a small table sat between the creaky wood framed windows. On top of the low table was a box of tissues and an electric suction machine. The smaller supplies were tucked into the drawers of the tables, and the larger one's hidden in the closet. There was a rocking chair.

I turned on a table lamp and led her to the rocking chair. I brought her the box of tissues. I asked her if she wanted some water or juice. She refused but I could tell she was just being polite. I went to the kitchen and brought back a glass of water anyway. She had wiped her eyes and the crying had stopped. I told her everything was alright, drink the water, and that I would be right back.

I ran back through the kitchen and to the room at the top of the stairs where everyone else was sleeping, in their clothes, ready to be woken up for a birth. Lumpy figures were scattered around the carpeted floor with pillows under their heads and light blankets rumpled over them. No birth I told them, but come downstairs anyway.

I went back to the birth room and sat on the floor in front of the rocking chair.

"*Tiene hambre?*" Are you hungry? It was just past midnight and I knew she had been walking for hours.

"*No, gracias.*" She would say no to anything I offered, not wanting to be more of a bother than she thought she was already being. The three other sleepy midwives came in.

"What's going on?" They wanted to know.

"I'm not sure." I motioned for them to sit down. They sat on the floor next to me and we all looked up at the sniffling woman slowly rocking the chair.

More crying and sorry and how nice we all are and that she came here because she knew we would understand. She knew we would help.

We all looked at each other not knowing what she was talking about. Then, like story time in kindergarten when the teacher announces the title of the book and shows the first picture to the anxious kids spread out around her feet, my new acquaintance Celia Carrillo began to tell her story.

She's from a little ranching town deep in Mexico. Has never seen a city as big as El Paso or Juarez on the Mexican side.

Lives in this little town with her husband and his family; his parents, his sisters and brothers, and her children.

Three young children. She misses them so much. Never separated before.

Figured out she was pregnant but didn't tell anyone.

The other pregnancies she was happy. This time only worried.

All children are God's children, right? He loves them all. No matter how they start.

Can't be a sin. It can't.

This child came from love.

God loves all children, right?

God will forgive her, but her husband won't, she reasoned.

He would beat her. Try to kill the baby. Keep her from her other children.

She had to leave before she started to get big. Before anyone suspected.

The only way to save the baby.

The only way to be a mother to the children she already had.

Go to the border and work at a factory for a while, she would say. Make money. Lots of people do it. A sacrifice to better her family.

Her mother-in-law and sister-in-law could watch the kids.

It would be so much money it would be worth it.

Finally her husband agreed.

One bus, then another, and another.

Finally in Juarez. But now what?

A church. They would help her.

They were so nice. They understood. Had seen this many times before.

Lots of people wanted new babies. Good people. They would arrange everything. The baby would be American. It was the best for everyone.

She was so relieved. Everything was going to work out.

In a few weeks she was living with them. Lupe Valdez. Her husband. Their two boys. In El Paso. The United States!

It was just like the church people said it would be. A husband and wife and their two teenaged boys. The boys didn't speak Spanish, but the husband and wife did. They wanted to have another, but couldn't. They had a nice house on the edge of El Paso. They went to church. This child would be spoiled. The final baby they had been waiting for. Maybe a girl, but it didn't matter either way.

She had her own room and she ate meals with the family. They arranged for her to have her baby at the clinic. Better than a hospital, they said. Less formal. No need to show identification. They paid the whole fee. But they wanted her to pretend her name was the name of the wife, and that she was married to the husband. That way the birth certificate wouldn't need to be changed. No messing with lawyers and a legal adoption. At first it was hard to say the wrong name when she came to appointments, but eventually she got used to it.

The family was nice to her. At first. She was going to be with them for five months and the wife suggested that she could help out around the house. That seemed fair, and she wanted to be busy. Helping to make dinner and clear the dishes turned into straightening up around the house, which turned into washing the teenaged boys' laundry and cleaning their messy rooms, which turned into being a live-in maid with a list of chores given in the morning and the requirement the chores would be done by the evening.

Initially the meals were good. There was so much more food than she was used to. Meat at every meal. Pots overflowing. The refrigerator always full. That was fortunate because being pregnant she was hungry all the time. But then as time went on the husband started to complain about how much money they were spending on groceries. How feeding her was like feeding two people (which it was). And then the wife started to limit what she ate. Enough, but not too much. She could have one serving of dinner, but no seconds. She could have one glass of milk at each meal, but not two. The boys could have as much as they wanted, but that was different. She would watch as they refilled their milk glasses two or three times at dinner. She knew that milk was important for the baby, and she wanted to drink more, but what could she do.

The baby would be okay wouldn't it?

And the boys were mean. Well, they were nice at first treating her as a guest, but then they started to make fun of her. Say things in English louder and louder, knowing she couldn't understand, and then laughing. And they lived far from town. There was no where to walk to except other houses in the neighborhood. They didn't want her going outside because the neighbors would be suspicious about the baby. So she stayed in the house. Cleaning and doing laundry. And having the boys laugh at her. And being hungry between meals. But they took her to her appointments at the clinic. They had to make sure the baby was okay.

She loved the appointments. Sitting in the crowded waiting room with the other mothers, new babies, and chatty families. And then her appointment. She would leave the wife, "her friend," in the waiting room and be alone. We would talk to her, smile, touch her, and best of all, let her listen to the baby's heart. She wanted to tell us but she was afraid. They had told her they had spent a lot of money on her. That if things didn't work out she would have to pay them back. They would call the police. She might even go to jail. She thought being a midwife looked so wonderful. We all seemed so happy. Like we really liked the work. And each other. It was like we were sisters. And it was all women. The students, the staff midwives, the secretaries, even the midwife who ran the whole clinic. We all knew so much and working with birth was such special work. God's work. She really did want to tell us.

As the baby got bigger she started to wonder if she was doing the right thing. If these people were really the right people to raise this baby. Her baby. God's baby. She knew she couldn't raise the baby herself, but she needed to make sure that it was raised right. Raised by good people. Loving people. People who would let a pregnant woman drink as much milk as she wanted.

She started to memorize the roads that the wife took to the appointments. Going to the clinic was the only time she was allowed out of the house. They weren't taking her to church anymore. That was only for the first few weeks. After a few Sundays they saw her talking to one of the other women. They didn't want her making any friends. They wanted that baby for their own and no one was going to interfere.

She wanted to get away, but the time never seemed right. But for the last few days she felt the baby moving down. She'd had that feeling with her other babies. She knew it was getting close. She had to leave soon if she was going to leave at all.

It seemed that someone was always home. She could tell they made sure not to leave her alone. The wife started asking her if she felt like labor was close. She would always say no even though she knew it was. Her back ached all the time. She couldn't take long steps without feeling that dull pinch down in front.

She waited until it was dark. Until she was sure everyone was asleep. She knew she only had one chance and she had to get away without anyone hearing.

We had all been listening in silence. We couldn't believe the story we were hearing. There were specific Spanish words here and there we couldn't understand, but we all knew enough to figure out the basic story. She could have stopped right there and I probably wouldn't have cried. I would have been sad, concerned, and certainly angry, but I wouldn't have cried. But then she told us exactly how she left the house.

The tears came to my eyes first. As poor as my Spanish was, it was better than everyone else's in the room. Of all of us sitting at her feet, only I knew that *ventana* was Spanish for window.

We put her to bed in the smallest birth room. The one that would be used only if the other two larger ones became occupied. Celia was afraid of the man and his wife. How mad they would be when they discovered she was gone. We promised we wouldn't tell them she was here. We wouldn't let them in if they came. We would tell them through the locked door to come back in the morning during regular hours.

By then we would have figured everything out we assured Celia. I was a lawyer, I told her. Yes, I said *abogada*. You heard right. I'm a lawyer *and* a midwife. I would help however I could. And yes, there was most certainly someone out there who would want her baby and would take care of it the way she wanted. Owing to my bumpy Spanish, she thought I had someone specific in mind when I said this.

"A midwife?" she asked hopefully. No. Well, I don't know. Well, maybe, but that's not what I meant. We were clearly her heroes.

We stayed up most of the night discussing what to do. When the clinic opened in the morning and the director arrived, the door closed to the meeting and the students were left outside.

Celia had fallen asleep shortly after we left her. She was awake and I asked her about breakfast. She said she wasn't hungry, but I walked to a take out restaurant anyway and got her a plate with eggs, beans, fried potatoes, warm tortillas rolled up in aluminum foil, and a big Styrofoam cup of milk.

It had been decided at the meeting that she would stay at one of the staff midwife's homes and deliver there. Surely when the family figured out she was gone they would come to the clinic or call. But what would they say? Was she there having her baby? Her husband, if he really was her husband, should already know. The same if he came by. The wife, her "friend" who gave her rides to the appointments, didn't have any right to be told any medical information. If she wanted to know what was going on with the pregnancy she should just call her friend and ask, we would tell her.

The fee for the birth had already been paid. The refund policy said that if a woman didn't end up delivering at the clinic the fee would be returned to her. We all knew that the husband and wife had actually paid the fee, but it was under Celia's name, or what we were all led to believe was her name, so the refund would go to her.

After breakfast Celia was hurried out of the clinic to the midwife's house where she would be staying. This midwife had an extra room, no children, and could reschedule her work days at the clinic until after the baby came. She would be able to take care of Celia and be sure to be home when she went into labor. Adoption agencies have lists of people waiting for a healthy newborn.

No one from the family came in, but the husband called later that day wondering if his wife was having her baby. When they woke up that morning and saw she was gone they must have panicked. Did she go to a neighbor? A church? The police? Back to Mexico? Who did she talk to and what did she say.

The husband said he was out of town for business. How else would he explain not knowing where his wife was?

He was told the truth; she had come in, told us she was not going to be delivering at the clinic, and was no longer a client. No she didn't say anything else. It's not really our business anyway. She can have her baby where ever she wants. If we get a request from another midwife or doctor for her records of course we'll provide them. And yes, the refund was given directly to her; the patient. That's our policy Sir. She was given a receipt and it's all detailed there. I'm sure you can just look at that. And yes it is a lot of money. (Just about what someone would make if they worked in a factory on the border for six months, we all took pleasure in realizing.)

The next few days at the clinic were tense every time the phone rang or someone came to the door, which was a lot. As each day passed we relaxed a little more and made reassuring arguments to each other that they would have called or come in by now if they were ever going to. We were right and we never heard from him or his real wife again.

Within a week Celia had delivered at the midwife's house and the very next day boarded a bus back to her little town in Mexico. She was tired from having just given birth, and normally we wouldn't recommend traveling on a long uncomfortable bus for days, but she wanted to get home as soon as she could. She couldn't wait to get back to her children.

When Celia was ready to leave the midwife's house, the midwife called to the clinic and asked if a student was available to come to her house and take Celia to the bus station. She or her husband would take Celia themselves, but they were busy taking care of the new baby. *Their* new baby. Celia was right, there was a midwife who would love and care for her baby just the way she herself would have.

When the student hung up the phone and then asked who could drive Celia to the bus station, there were three of us sitting around the table chatting. We were between appointments on a slow day. I wasn't busy and could easily have gone. Instead I said nothing. Another student broke the silence and said she would do it. I mumbled something about checking the supplies in the birth rooms. I knew Celia felt close to me and would want to see me again, but I was afraid to see her. I didn't know what I would say. I'm most comfortable being social when being social means that I'm giving out answers.

When I'm being a midwife I check your blood pressure and tell you the numbers. You ask me questions about what the numbers mean and I tell you. It looks like we're having a conversation. You even feel like we're having a conversation. I talk, then you talk, then I talk. Afterward you might tell you friend that you really enjoyed your appointment. That you get along so well with your midwife and can really talk to her.

You think we're having a conversation. But we're not. You are asking and I am telling. That's exactly how I want it. There won't be any surprises where I might have to talk about my feelings, or have my intelligence challenged. When I'm talking about pregnancy to a midwife patient, I have all the answers. At least you are convinced I do. Just like when I'm talking about the law to a client. There are two people talking, but it's not a conversation.

For months I could feel Celia's belly and tell her the position of her baby without a moment of hesitation or social discomfort. Just a few days ago I carefully explained why we didn't have any legal obligation to her fake husband to tell him where she was. I was the model of confidence in those situations. But just the thought of driving her to the bus when she could begin talking about anything at all made me want to run away, like she had from that family. I would balance on a wobbly chair to climb out a window and then hold my breath and jump the final feet to the ground. I would walk for miles at night on a highway, practically bare foot and without a penny, a bit of food, or a sip of water, just to avoid the chance that she might ask me about my feelings. I know how to stop a woman from bleeding to death when a piece of placenta is trapped inside of her uterus, but I wouldn't know what to say to Celia to comfort her if she started to cry about leaving her new baby. I knew I didn't want any part of it.

My Spanish would be imperfect but that didn't bother me at all. What I was afraid of was doing something that would leave Celia disappointed with me. I was afraid she would stop liking me. Stop thinking I was smart and nice and helpful, and whatever else she thought of me. I would rather avoid the goodbye than risk having her opinion of me lowered. She would probably only want the opportunity to thank me. But strangely that was a problem too.

She would say 'Gracias' and then get on the bus leaving me without the opportunity to do anything more for her. I couldn't repay her gift, the 'thank you,' by measuring her uterus, or by bringing her food, or by promising to protect her as her lawyer. She would give me a gift and I wouldn't have one to give back. As soon as the "Gracias" would leave her mouth it would zoom through the air and stick to me like an arrow pushing into a bull's eye, no time to stand to the side or get away. I couldn't let her appreciation of me be the last event to occur between us.

It would take another ten years until I felt worthy of accepting thanks. Until that time I thought that I had an obligation to help everyone who asked. I was a 'giver,' not a 'taker.' I said "yes" to everyone who wanted to hire me as their lawyer. I thought I had to. I had so many cases opened that I had to put an extra filing cabinet in the hall just to hold all the papers. I was bouncing from court to court with only the driving time in between to prepare. I would be nursing my infant son at my desk with a client sitting across from me telling me about his cocaine use and how the amount he had when he was arrested was just enough to support his habit, not extra that he was going to sell. My son's eyes would slide closed and he would stop sucking. I would call my secretary in and she would take him from me, holding him at her desk while he slept, answering the phone and writing down messages with one hand. I was overwhelmed.

After finally having the strength to say "no" to someone with criminal charges, I slyly watched out of my office window as he got in his car. I felt awful. Like I had left him floating on an iceberg. Alone. Cold. And a hungry shark approaching. I crouched down just at the edge of the window so I could see him but he couldn't see me. He slowly took his sunglasses off their special hook on the visor, put them on his face, looked at himself in the rearview mirror, combed his hair with his fingers, and then backed out of the parking space.

Watching him watch himself in the mirror I felt instantly better. Unburdened. A responsibility melted away. The guilt of saying "no" was gone. I realized that nothing in his life changed because I didn't take his case. He didn't die. He didn't get taken to jail. His home didn't get swirled around inside a tornado. His girlfriend didn't dump him. Coming to see if he could hire me was just another chore he had that day; pay the gas bill, get the mail, go to the auto store to buy a new leather steering wheel cover, and go to Sheri's office and look sad when I tell her about all my problems and try to convince her that she is the only one who can help me, and then promise to pay her but not actually do it.

When I saw he had taken the trouble to put his sunglasses on their little hook before he came in for his appointment, I realized that he was as equally concerned about avoiding scratches as he was about having me take his case. He didn't think his future depended solely on me, so why did I? I stopped thinking about him the second I couldn't see his car anymore. Just then I knew that I didn't have to give just because there was someone willing to take. It was okay to say no, and not only that, but it was also okay to accept what others wanted to give to me; including thanks.

When the other student got back from the bus station she said Celia had asked for me. The student promised she would relay to me a message from Celia; "*gracias.*"

9

Marina's Baby Cuando

I'm rubbing Marina's back. She has been in labor for so many hours I've lost count. I could look at her chart and figure it out, but what's the point. It was light out when it started and now it's dark. I'm with her until she delivers. Whenever that is. When I examined her just a few minutes ago I was so hoping I could tell her she was ten centimeters. Ready to push. We would both smile and be magically infused with the energy of knowing that this would all be over soon. She was seven. I tried to smile when I told her, not wanting her to catch my disappointment. This isn't her first baby and I keep wondering why it's taking so long. She's wondering too.

"*Cuando*?" When? She keeps asking. Not really asking me, although I'm the only one in the room, but just asking.

She is standing next to a standard medical examination table; narrow, elevated at the head, and stirrups that fold out at the end. A roll of white paper attached near the top. In this birth clinic most women deliver on the queen sized bed, or squatting on a birth stool. In the many months I have been here I have only seen this examination table used for one thing in labor; leaning against.

It's hot. The ceiling fan is quietly whirring the heavy El Paso air around the cozy room. If we were lucky enough for there to be a breeze, it would billow the lace curtains on the tall wood framed windows. But for the box of gloves on the nightstand, the room looks like a lived-in bedroom with slightly mismatched furniture. The oxygen tank and other equipment is stored in the closet or tucked into the drawers of the dresser.

Marina grabs the side of the examination table and leans forward as another contraction starts. She breathes hard. We are both exhausted. It seems that we've been through hundreds of contractions together just like this one. That head was so high up when I examined her I just know we're going to do this many more times before the baby's ready to come out. I wonder if I'm going to be able to stay awake—acutely aware of how selfish that thought is.

I'm standing behind Marina and have been gently massaging her shoulders and neck. At the height of the contraction she reaches her hand behind to try to rub her lower back. I quickly replace her hand with both of mine and press my palms hard against the center of her lower back, trying to push the baby's head off her spine.

"*Aqui?*" Here? I ask quietly.

She nods with relief. I press my palms a little harder against her back. Then we both hear it. A loud pop like when you twist a certain way and something in your back cracks. Painlessly. The sound came from under my hands. What did I push?

Maybe it was just the surprise, or the quiet all around us, the unexpected break in the routine, but the pop seemed really loud. I pull my hands away to look at Marina's back. I don't know what I think I will see. Marina too turns her head trying to look, gazing down over her shoulder. The 'pop' really was loud.

The only noise in those seconds we are both looking is the churning of the ceiling fan, until—SPLAT! A burst of water hits the floor. Marina's pink slippers are soaked in amniotic fluid. My shoes and the few inches of bare legs below my cropped pants are dotted with fluid too.

We both look up from the small puddle on the floor and then, before either of us can say anything Marina leans forward towards the examining table and bears down uncontrollably.

"*Tengo ganas! Tengo ganas!*" I have the urge to push!

"*Muy Buen!*" Very good! I say gently, and then border Spanish for *push:* "*Pushele!*"

That pop must have been something moving out of the way. The edge of a bony vertebra? A little ball of tight muscle? Who knows, but now the baby is moving down unobstructed like it's been trying to do all this time. I picture a line of traffic finally able to move now that the stalled car has been pushed to the side of the road.

I squat down behind Marina to look for the top of the head. Nothing yet and Marina has stopped pushing. She's taking loud, deep breaths. The contraction is ending. I'm not supposed to deliver a baby without the supervising midwife and two other students in the room; one to assist and one to take notes in the chart.

With the next contraction, and the push that will go with it, the baby will probably come. This is my only chance to leave and tell everyone else to come. I run in the hall and shout up the stairs where everyone is sleeping that a baby's coming. NOW! I don't wait for a response, but just run back to the room. I have been woken up this way before. The "sleep" in this circumstance is more like a rest; fully dressed and one subconscious eye always open.

Marina is standing next to the examination table gripping onto the edge. Her eyes are squeezed shut and her mouth curled up at the edges. I encourage her to push when she has the urge.

"*Eschuce su cuerpo.*" Listen to your body.

I put on a pair of gloves and squat behind her, ready to catch the baby. I can see the head pushing Marina's skin out of the way as it as it moves down towards my hands. I hear the door to my right click open and the quick footsteps of the supervising midwife and two students as they spread out around the room, collecting the items necessary for the birth. I am aware of them moving around behind me but I keep my hands and eyes on the head. My only job is to catch the baby.

I hear the stainless steel bowl filled with the birth instruments clink down on the wood floor next to me. We bring the instruments to the Mother, not the other way. The supervising midwife is crouching behind me reminding me to keep pressure on the top of the head to keep Marina's skin from tearing. In this position, the mother standing and me delivering the baby from behind her, I have to push the emerging head *upwards* to prevent a tear. With the mother on the bed and me delivering the baby from in front of her, the head has to be pushed *down*. Everything is backwards and it's hard for me to reorient.

During the next push I put pressure on the head in the correct direction and it slowly comes all the way out, just like it should. I'm sure Marina let out a scream, but I stopped hearing that many births ago. I am just looking anxiously for the head to turn easily to the side, a sign that the baby's shoulders aren't stuck. It does, and thankfully, they aren't. That's one complication I will not have to correct. I gently press and pull to deliver one shoulder, and then the other. There is a good two feet between the slippery baby and the floor. I keep one hand in the notch of the neck, and grab around the ankles with the other.

One of the other students is crouched down next to me with a towel unfolded over her hands. I place the baby into the towel and she rubs it dry, eliciting the familiar first cry; soft and stuttered for a few seconds and then loud and constant as the baby announces that it will be staying. Marina is looking over her shoulder down at her baby. Her skin on her face is smooth again, the closed eyes open and the tight mouth relaxed into a smile.

The umbilical cord is running from the baby's belly up into Marina. We can only move the baby a few inches either direction without pulling on the cord. I gently put my two fingers around the cord and I can feel it pulsing. I could cut it now for convenience sake, but that would cheat the baby out of the last bits of blood running to it. We all shuffle back a few feet to the end of the bed, moving as a group like a giant amoeba.

Marina lays back on the bed, the baby being held close to her side by the assistant. I lift Marina's leg to keep it off the cord that is snaked beneath it, and the baby is passed under her thigh and placed on Marina's stomach. A dry towel is wrapped around the baby, a hat placed on its head, and a stethoscope on its chest. "One forty" is called out. A normal heart rate, and we can all hear the crying. The baby is fine, and is now the responsibility of the assistant. I am in charge of the placenta.

I watch the cord coming out of Marina's vagina. If more of it starts to come out, accompanied by a small trickle of blood, it is a sign everything is normal and the placenta is ready to deliver. If blood comes out, but it's more than a trickle, then it's a sign of a hemorrhage. It is a subtle, but very serious difference.

I have come to understand that my job as a midwife includes keeping a mental checklist of abnormal events and when, chronologically, each one would happen. Once the time for each has passed, I cross it off my list and watch for the next. Only when everything is checked off can I relax.

Three and a half hours have gone by. I have made scrambled eggs and fried potatoes for Marina and helped her eat it in bed. I have cleaned the dried blood off her thighs with a warm washcloth. I have helped her change into a fresh nightgown and washed her other one. I have worked her clean pair of underwear up her legs and placed on it a sanitary pad I swiped from the clinic, instead of the tattered bleached rag she brought with her. I have gathered her long hair off of her face and secured it in a clip I found in her bag while looking for the nightgown and underwear. I have placed the pillows around her just right so that she can breastfeed without having to strain her back. I get her juice and hold the glass while she lies in bed holding her baby and sips from the straw I have put between her lips. I have examined the baby from head to toe and told her the weight in grams and the length in centimeters, so that it will have some meaning to her. I have put antibiotic drops in the eyes and a shot of vitamin K in the thigh. I have explained to Marina how to clean the bit of cord coming out of the baby's belly so it doesn't get infected. How often to feed the baby (don't look at the clock, look at the baby. When she sticks out her tongue and turns her head, she's hungry). How to know if the baby is getting enough. I have told Marina she needs to rest even if she somehow has some energy. How much bleeding is too much and a sign that she's being too active. Over and over I ask her to tell me what I can do for her.

When they both fall asleep, I look through the chart. I am sitting in a rocking chair at the side of the bed. At her first appointment she was asked for her occupation. The word "clean" was written by the midwife in the answer space, which I assume means that every day she crosses the border from the cardboard houses, prostitution, and general disorder of poverty in Juarez, to the relative wealth and splendor of El Paso. Here she washes someone else's floors, cleans someone else's toilets, and folds someone else's laundry. After the loud scolding she once got while standing in someone else's kitchen, she also wraps a wet cloth around her pinky finger and drags it down the tiny space of counter between the back of the kitchen sink and the wall. She will probably be back cleaning houses ten hours a day within a week of giving birth.

I flip through the papers in the chart and check what time it was that I examined Marina and she was seven centimeters dilated. Then I see how much time passed until the baby was born. I'm so tired I have to count on my fingers. Eleven minutes. Amazing. She's amazing. I'm glad I got to take care of her.

10

Black Boys in Boston

It had just gotten dark and I was walking back from the subway station to my apartment in South Boston. This was my first apartment after graduating from law school. The neighborhood wasn't the best, but it wasn't so dangerous that I wouldn't walk there after dark, obviously, but I made sure to notice what was happening around me and not to waste time getting home.

As I left the subway station and walked my usual route on the deserted area beneath the curvy overpasses of the highway leading into downtown Boston, and the various entrance and exit ramps, I saw a police car parked ahead, lit only by the distant street lights. My first thought was relief.

I used to walk home on the other side of the subway station, going to the previous apartment I lived in. My home during my last year of law school. I once came home and saw what I thought was a dead body in the bushes next to the stairs of the triple decker apartment house. I stared at the fat white guy, somewhere in his twenties and didn't see him move. At all. I yelled at him. Still nothing.

I ran faster than I thought I could on the cracked sidewalk that lined the busy main street until I got to the police sub station a few blocks away. When I burst in I was so out of breath from sprinting that I couldn't talk. I stood in front of the desk breathing hard and staring at the officer behind it. He asked me questions I could answer by nodding my head.

"Are you okay?"

"Are you injured?"

"Is someone following you?"

"Is there someone outside who needs help?"

Finally I could get out a few words and what I said energized the lazy crew sitting around and talking.

"Dead." "Body." "Mosely." "Street." And I pointed the direction I had come from.

I was pushed into a police car. Lights flashing and siren blaring, and three or four others just like it behind us. I got out and pointed. One of the officers kicked the body and it groaned. Everyone relaxed. Just a drunk. I felt awful for the false alarm, but the police didn't seem to mind. A few of the officers made the best of it by kicking the guy until they got him up, pushing him hard against the wall, and then roughly sending him staggering on his way, scolding him for scaring this nice young lady; me.

So I knew there was a police station relatively near by the subway stop and I thought that tonight the cops had decided to park under the highway as a little neighborhood patrol.

As I walked, I saw that there were people at the back of the car. Two in police uniforms, and two not. Once I got closer I made out the whole scene. Two skinny black teenaged boys standing at the back of the police car, in their boxer shorts and nothing else. It was a warm summer night, but not that warm. They had their hands on the trunk and were slightly bent over. Their clothes were on the ground around them. The cops were both white. One had a sneaker in his hand and was shaking it upside down.

Everyone looked as they saw me approach, surprised by the foot traffic no doubt.

I quickly figured out that the cops were searching the boys. I felt uncomfortable, embarrassed for the boys, and planned to walk by without looking. I thought about the news stories for the last few months about strip searches on suspected gang members. How it had been overused, violating the rights of those searched, and was basically just harassment. The Mayor and the Police Chief had announced some new policy or other that was supposed to make it stop. I hadn't paid too much attention.

As I walked towards my apartment, a path that would lead right in front of the police car, I started thinking back to my criminal law class.

I started to quiz myself; when is it legal to do a search? There is a search that an officer can do if he's talking with someone who looks scary and he wants to make sure the guy doesn't have any weapons. But that only lets the officer do a pat down, over the clothes. Having just studied two months straight for the Bar exam I remembered it's called a 'Terry Search.' Mr. Terry, from Ohio, was searched and his situation made it all the way to the U.S. Supreme Court.

And then they can do a full search, in pockets, under the clothes, if the person is under arrest. That's clearly the kind of search these boys are undergoing, so they must be under arrest. But if they are, then why didn't the cops just take them to the police station that's so close to us I was able to run there?

Maybe they're not under arrest. But if they're not under arrest then the cops can only do a pat down search, over the clothes. And if they are under arrest, then they should be at the police station. I'm almost at the police car and I'm sure of it; the search is illegal. At least, I'm pretty sure.

I slow down my pace as I near the police car. When I'm directly in front of it, I stop. The officer without the shoe walks out from behind the police car and tells me that everything is fine and I should keep going. He has a wide smile for me. If we weren't so far apart he would pat my back and reassure me that he was taking care of everything.

I don't move. Again he tells me that everything's okay and I can keep on my way. The smile is gone. When I still don't leave he trades a glance with the other officer, the one holding the shoe.

I tell him I know I can leave, thank you, but I want to stay and watch. This is a public area after all.

Now both officers are sure that I might be trouble. The officer without the shoe, the one who told me I could go, comes around the front of the car, his hand on the top of his holster. The reassuring smile he showed me before is now permanently gone. I look at the boys. They have their heads up from looking at the trunk and they are looking at me. We catch each others eyes and stare for a few seconds too long. They might as well have tape over their mouths and their hands tied behind their backs. They know anything they say or do will only make things worse.

The cop is no longer asking me to leave, he is telling me to leave. This is THE moment. The turning point when I can either leave and we all agree to pretend like nothing ever happened, or I stay and become officially against the police, and treated like it.

I hesitate and then, glancing at the boys in the distance behind the car, their eyes wide waiting for my next move, I announce that I'm going to stay. Stay and watch.

Silence.

The officer in front looks back at the officer with the shoe.

The officer with the shoe looks at the boys.

The boys look at down at the trunk, and then at each other.

Eventually, everyone is looking at me.

It seems like the next person to speak wins some amount of control.

"This is an illegal search."

The boys are wide eyed, staring at what looks like a crazy young white girl in shorts, a t-shirt, sneakers, and long hair in a bouncy pony tail. Talking back to a cop. They know better, why don't I? The cops clearly believe they can do whatever they want to young black boys. I'm hopeful that my white skin will keep me safe. But maybe I need more.

"This is an illegal search." I say again.

"What do you know about it?" The closer cop says half laughing and shaking his head.

"I'm a lawyer." I force out, making an effort to keep my voice strong. The cop with the shoe doesn't move but just stares. I motion towards the boys, "if you're going to do a strip search they need to be under arrest. And if they're under arrest they should be at the police station." The boys are standing up a little, almost smiling. I'm really hoping I have this right.

The front cop looks back at the cop standing near the boys and they nod in silent agreement. The front cop takes a few steps closer to me. I want his name.

"What's your name?"

And the other officer. I want his name too.

"And your name too," I say a little louder towards the cop by the trunk. I'm shaking, but they can't see it. I'm careful to keep my voice steady. I open my purse and dig for a pen and scrap of paper. Neither one says anything.

I take a step closer to the cop nearest me so I can look at his badge. He takes his hand off his holster and pulls his badge off. He puts it in his pocket. The one in the back does the same. I'm standing with my pen and crumpled cash register receipt in my hands.

"We're conducting an investigation here." The front cop tells me, "You're interfering with our investigation." He reaches behind his back and touches his handcuffs so they jingle. I stand still. I know if I don't leave soon I'll be arrested. But I don't want to leave because then they've won. And that means the boys have lost. It's me and the boys against the police, three against two. We outnumber them. We should be the winners. But the boys can't participate, so really it's one against two. The police outnumber me. This isn't fair and I don't know how to fix it.

The rules from the Red Cross class I took flash into my mind. If you see someone that needs CPR you don't have any obligation to stop and help, but if you choose to, once you start CPR you are only allowed to stop for two reasons: more qualified help arrives, or you're too exhausted to continue.

Even though the boys don't need first aid, I feel in my heart the same obligation as if I'm doing CPR. In this situation, more qualified help isn't going to arrive, so I think I can only stop when I'm too exhausted to continue. I can't be there yet. I need to figure out a way to either make the officers stop the search, or be held responsible for doing it in the first place.

I don't think I can make them stop. If anything they're going to very effectively make me stop trying. Later I can make a complaint to their superiors about what I've seen, but how can I do that if I don't know their names? There must be one more thing I can do before I give up. Before I'm too tired to continue with the stop-the-illegal-search- CPR.

I run my eyes around the whole scene again looking for something I can use: two angry cops without name tags, two half naked embarrassed boys, a pile of clothes scattered around the back of a police car. That's it— the car! There must be a way to trace the officers through their car. Some kind of sign out sheet somewhere.

I move directly in front of the car and write down the license plate number with my shaky hand, making sure the officer sees me do it, and then I feel satisfied. I know that I have done everything I can. For now. I can leave. Not leaving because I'm giving up, but because I no longer need to be here. Here in the officers' faces. Here staring at the boys in their underwear. Here isolated under the highway in the dark with my should-be-protectors as my enemies. Here is no longer where I need to be.

I announce I'm ready to leave. The boys stare, mouths dropped open, as I walk off, holding my back straight and not looking back. I shake all the way home.

The second I get in the door I grab my criminal law textbook and look through the part on searches. I was right after all. The search was illegal.

The next day I write the letter to the Mayor. I use the benefit of all my years of education to put down on paper a coherent, detailed account of what I saw, and the legal analysis that goes with it. I realize that being able to say I am a lawyer is something that matters. Something that will make my complaint letter be taken more seriously than the other hundreds the Mayor must get each week. Maybe it's not fair that my lawyer voice is louder than others, but it's the best way I can help, so I'm going to use it.

First a week goes by. Then another. Then I stop being so eager when I check the mail. Then a month goes by. Then another month. I replay the night, thinking of all the ways I could have stayed and done more. How I should have stayed and done more. Done something. How they never would have arrested me. How I was wrong that I could help the boys by writing a letter. That the only way to help was to stay and keep arguing, and I didn't do it. I only cared about myself, about not getting arrested. I'm just as bad as the cops, putting me first and the boys last. They looked at me and asked for help. I started to help and then stopped in the middle. Worse than not starting at all. You don't *have* to help, but if you choose to, then you *have* to finish. The boys probably got worse treatment because of what I did. Now I wish I hadn't been there at all.

Why hadn't my subway train been full so I had to take the next one ten minutes later? If I had only spent another half minute at the token booth. Let someone walk ahead of me at the turnstile. Stopped to tie my shoe, wipe my nose, put on lip gloss. Then I would have been walking through the parking lot when everything was already over. Too late to do the nothing I did and too late to even know there was something I was supposed to worry about.

Then, after I had given up, it came. Finally. Here it was and I was afraid to open it, but only for a minute. As I push my finger under the edge of the flap and tear across the top of the envelope I'm shaking almost as much as that night under the highway.

It isn't the Mayor who deals with this, but the police chief, so my letter was transferred there. And then there's a special division that does the investigation. And then a formal hearing; one for each officer. A lot of administrative rules and deadlines, the letter explains. The process takes time. But thank you for your patience. Without concerned citizens like you. Since you lodged the complaint we are obliged to inform you of the result....

And then the good part. The part that made the months of waiting disappear. The part that made me know I hadn't walked away too soon. The part that convinced me I was right to make those boys my business. The part that was like a door slamming on the part of that night that had been left slightly ajar.

The investigation is complete. Of course the specifics are confidential, but some information is public. The law applies to everyone. All officers held to a certain standard, no exceptions. Behavior against policy. Formal discipline. A negative effect on any future promotions. A permanent mark in the personnel records....

I read it a second time. Trying to tell if the boys knew. I hoped they did. I wondered if they were part of the investigation. If they got an apology. If they knew I actually did something after I walked away. That I didn't just leave them and decide to keep their problems from becoming mine.

I imagine that the boys and I are reading the letter at the same time. Me, as I am in the lobby of my apartment building, the boys back on that night, at the trunk of the car. Laughing. Waving the letter at the cops like the burning log my father once pulled from the fire and waved at the bear who came into our campsite. The cops stumble back from their car, like the frightened bear, and the boys take their time getting dressed amid their satisfied laughter.

11

So That's Where Babies Come From

For a long time I wondered when it was I first became interested in birth. Many midwives describe being "called" to the work. That they always felt inside that birth was their "path." That they saw a birth and just knew. Or they had their own baby, either in the hospital and knew there was something better, or with a midwife and knew that was the something better. I had none of this. No vision. No dreams. No spiritual phone endlessly ringing until the day.... At least nothing that I'm willing to admit to. I live in the here and now. If I can't see it, touch it, hear it, or smell it, I'm not interested.

All those kids that wanted to be astronauts, floating off in outer space somewhere - not interested. What was it like when the dinosaurs roamed the earth? Don't know, don't care. I like shopping. I like touching the shirt, smelling the perfume, holding the little card with the earrings on it up to the side of my face and twisting to see in the mirror, looking at the designs on the boxes of tissues and deciding which I like best. Eating is good too.

More times than I can count, during a labor when I am in a dimly lit room getting ready to put my fingers inside the mom to check her dilation, someone offers to turn on the light. When I say I don't need it, they think about it for a few seconds and laugh, embarrassed. But it's not so crazy. Even though I'm not looking with my eyes, I see in my mind a picture of what I am feeling. Just like I'm looking at the new shirt, or earrings, I see the perfectly round edges of the circle formed by the opened cervix, the hard head in the center like a bulls eye, the pink shiny skin of the uterus stretched up around it. Sometimes I even see the color of the hair I'm touching, but let's put that in the same locked box as me walking into the birth clinic the first day of school and recognizing the waiting room from a dream.

Before I started school to become a midwife I had never given birth myself or even been to a birth. I was the only one in my class who hadn't done one of the two. But I was also the only one in my class who was a lawyer. I had been interested in birth for years without really being sure why. When I quit my lawyer job in Boston I was faced with the choice of looking for another job or looking for another life. I decided on the latter.

The first strong memory I have of being attracted to birth came from the Boston Science Museum. Many Saturdays when I was a child my parents would take me and my sisters there. Instead of Chuck-E-Cheese for birthday parties, we would go to the Boston Science Museum with a car load of friends, and then eat dinner in Chinatown, the waiters teaching us how to use chopsticks. When I was little we would all stay together in the museum and see the boring stuff; the life sized displays of cavemen pointing spears at hairy animals, the gears that would interlock and turn when you pushed a button, the live snakes in glass containers (yikes!), and displays about chemical reaction that were more description than interesting stuff to look at.

Then there were the fun parts; the giant maze that a ball would run endlessly through, the display of telephones through the years from the first phone that Alexander Graham Bell spoke into, to the modern phones of 1975. There was the phone of the future that had a video screen. What if you're in bed looking terrible when you answer and it's the boy you like from school!

There was Spooky the Owl who must have been about two hundred years old, and would sit quietly on the museum man's arm while he pointed out the special gripping toenails that were good for grabbing unsuspecting mice, layers of feathers that kept the owl both cool and warm, and the head that doesn't really spin all the way around.

And there was the lightning room where there would be some long boring speech about science that I would daydream and fidget through and then the lights would dim and real lightning would snap across the room between two big towers. The ceiling was very high.

And there was the invisible woman with blue veins and miles of intestine. And the Archimedes water screw that you could use two hands to turn and see the blue colored water flow through the long tube. Even though that was pure science, it was hands on so I was able to tolerate it.

We would eat lunch in the cafeteria overlooking the Charles River. Hamburgers, pizza, french fries, jello. There was soda available, but we had to settle for chocolate milk. There must have been better food for the adults, but of course I don't remember that.

When we got a little older my father would let us go on our own through the museum and then meet back at the pendulum. "Meet here at 11:00."

Just inside the turnstiles at the museum entrance there was a large table with blocks the size of dominos set up on it in a big circle. A heavy brass pendulum was hung in the exact middle. The pendulum was slowly swinging from side to side between the small spaces between the blocks. The pendulum stayed on the same path, but every so often it would knock over a block. *Because even though the path of the pendulum wasn't moving, the earth was!* See why it's called the Science Museum?

We would take off in different directions. I would skip the boring stuff. As instructed, at 11:00 the whole family, except for my oldest sister, who was distracted somewhere else, giggling from a distance as some kid was being yelled at by his parents for running off, or walking too slowly, or touching, or not touching, or making a face at his sister, or claiming he didn't have to use the bathroom when two minutes later, when it was terribly inconvenient, he was asking to use the bathroom, would be at the pendulum reporting on what we had seen.

I was wandering around to my usual stops when I saw a special exhibit. Something that was only there temporarily, like King Tut's tomb, but without the gold. It was an exhibit on birth. It was probably called something like The Miracle of Life or Looking Inside the Womb. I can't remember exactly, but I knew I wanted to go in. Walls had been constructed in a sort of nautilus like roundness to make up the room. The entrance was at the opening of the shell. It was designed so that from outside the door you couldn't see anything that was inside. There was a sign at the door that said children under fourteen could not come in without an adult.

I paused outside the door, pretending I was looking at the display case with step by step instructions of how to build a battery. There wasn't any one at the door checking ages. I could always say I was fourteen if someone did ask and then, by way of explanation, say that I'm small for my age. This kept me from looking my truthful age of twelve so why not fourteen? I could wait until an adult walked in and trail behind, pretending like we were together. I could go and look around really fast and see as much as I could before someone noticed I was alone and young and dragged me out, holding my arm while they called my parents' names over the loudspeaker. Or I could just go in like I belonged there, keep very quiet, and hope no one noticed me. Finding my mother or father and asking them to go with me never occurred to me.

I walked in like I belonged and then did my best to be invisible. The walls did curve around like a shell. At the beginning, across from the entrance, were large pictures on the wall of weird floating jellyfish with red and blue wires around them. Despite the shape being wrong, I could tell they were definitely jelly fish. I had seen some dead ones splattered against the rocks on the beach at Cape Hatteras. I even got stung behind my knees when I was wading in the waves. As the pictures progressed, so did the odd lumps sticking out of the jellyfish. And the definition of the lumps became more apparent too. Arms, legs, a head. Oh.

There were informational placards beneath the pictures that declared the month of pregnancy and what exactly was developing. I just looked at the pictures and didn't bother much with the descriptions. I continued to walk around the curving wall until the pictures stopped. Month nine. Then, instead of pictures, there were round holes in the wall the width of paper towel tubes. Again an information placard underneath, but with smaller writing. Everybody else in the exhibit was much older. People were looking into the holes in the wall and then moving on to the next. Some people, mostly the men, looked at the first few and then walked away, going to the lung display in the center of the room. This must be the "fourteen and older" part. I willed myself completely invisible and casually walked ahead.

I stood on my toes and looked into the first hole. It was a picture of a woman and man walking into a hospital. The woman has long blond hair in two braids. The man has long hair too, but not long enough for braids. The woman is very pregnant. The next picture the woman is in a wheelchair being pushed by a nurse. Then she is in a hospital gown on her back in a skinny bed, an IV in her arm and surrounded by medical people in masks and gowns. Then we are at the end of the bed and her legs are in stirrups, with blue drapes completely covering them. We can see her shaved vagina, this was 1976, and the doctor's hand stretching it open to one side and inserting a needle. Now the doctor's hand is gone and something black and swirly is pushing her vagina open from the inside. I go through the progression of holes and see the doctor squeezing on the scissors as he cuts an episiotomy. The black swirly thing is out, it is a head with matted black hair. The doctor's gloved hands are pulling out the rest of the baby. The baby is hanging upside down from one of his hands and screwing up its face with a cry. The doctor is crinkling the edges of his mask with a smile. We can't see the mother's face past her bent knees. The episiotomy is being stitched with black thread and a curved needle. The baby is now clean and wrapped tightly in a blanket. A nurse is handing the baby to its mother, who is now in a different room, herself cleaned up and in a new gown, a huge smile on her face.

I am entranced. I go back and look in all the holes again, and then again. This is amazing. I can't believe I just saw a human being come out of another human being. That doctor must know so much to be in charge of something like that. How lucky he is to get to do that. How thankful the mother must be that he was *able* to do that; to get her baby out. That would really be something if I could ever know enough to do that.

I wonder what this is doing in the science museum? It isn't science. It's not really medicine either since no one is sick. I don't know what it is. I go through all the subjects I have in school: math, English, social studies, history, foreign language, art, music, gym. Study hall? Free time? Lunch? Homeroom? The fifteen minutes between school letting out and the buses arriving? There is no category for this, but still it exists. And unlike all the school subjects, I want to know all about it.

When we are waiting at the pendulum for the one missing sister, I don't tell what I saw. I don't want to get in trouble because of the age thing, but also I don't want to let anything escape. Not the feeling of amazement, not the wondering about how the doctor got the baby out, and certainly not the dream that maybe I could someday do that too. I know I'm probably not smart enough to be a doctor, and if I can't be a doctor how else could I do it? There's too much to sort out in my mind. The only thing I know for sure is that this needs to be a secret.

I say only that I saw the phones.

12

The Big American Dream

When I am remembering, my view is from behind the car, instead of in it. I am seeing myself sitting in the back seat of one of the many station wagons we had during my childhood. I am looking out the window as a group of boys run excitedly next to the slow moving car. My father is maneuvering the big blue Ford down a narrow bumpy road somewhere in Mexico; the big box of the tent trailer following behind. A crumpled map on the hot vinyl seat next to my father, showing, I suppose, the way to our next camping destination. I am just living in the moment wishing we were in a motel near Disneyland, like my normal friends.

The boys wear only shorts, have bare feet, and pad along single file between our car and the close, lopsided, brick walls on either side. I don't see any girls. The boys are trying to keep their hands pressed against the hot sides of the car as it moves carefully through the skinny, bumpy maze. They have huge white grins shining out from their dirt colored faces. It's like they have walked around a corner and seen the lights and rides of a giant amusement park where just yesterday there was an empty field with a falling down barn. But what has changed their day from ordinary to exciting, changed their moods from bored to elated, changed their view of the future from everyday nothing to exotic something, isn't an amusement park, it's just average America circa 1973; a big station wagon and a little blond girl, their same age, squinting out the sun as she peers at their faces from the back seat, her hand in a box of Cocoa Puffs.

I was a middle class girl from Connecticut on her eccentric father's idea of summer vacation. Just a month earlier I was wishing I could trade my hand-me-downs for the red, white and blue patchwork smock I saw in the Sears catalog. Then my clothes would be as nice, or if I was lucky, even *nicer*, than the other girls at school. I was wishing that I didn't have to share a room with my sister. I wanted a house so big that I could have my *own* bedroom where I could talk on the phone to my friends without anyone else in the house hearing my impassioned discourses on patchwork smocks from Sears. I wanted a backyard pool like our neighbor—and I didn't even like to swim—I just thought it would make the other kids think I was important. *And rich!*

The way these boys were looking at me I had a hundred smocks from Sears, my own giant bedroom with a pink princess phone, and the pool in our backyard wasn't the kind that was round with tilting blue plastic walls and a freestanding mini staircase pushed up to it, but the in-ground kind shaped like an 8. The way these boys looked at me, at the whole giant-gas-guzzling-pink-sparkly-barrettes-cooler-full-of-food-Etch-a-Sketch-ignored-on-the-seat-beside-me-home-away-from-home-tent-trailer-complete-with-couches-that-convert-into-comfortable-beds-and-a-miniature-sink-that-fills-with-a-hose-from-the-outside-and-actually-works, scene, I finally had all of the "my stuff is better than yours!" status that I had been dreaming about. I was quiet for a long time trying to figure out why it felt so awful.

Epilogue

A Recent Sunday
May, 2012

Tomorrow I have a criminal jury selection. Years ago, before I was a judge, that would have made me nervous. I would spend the night going over my questions to the jurors. Worrying about my client. Worrying about me. Worrying that my alarm wouldn't go off. Worrying about whether my car would start (why wouldn't it?). Basically, worrying about everything.

But now, I don't have to worry about anything, except maybe what time I'll get home. As the judge all I do is sit in the front of the court room, read all of the legal instructions, and watch the lawyers do the work. Occasionally I have to use some brain power to rule on objections, but mostly I'm relaxed to the point of boredom. It still bothers me when I see where the lawyers could be doing a better job. Or more accurately, how I would do it differently (and of course, in my mind, better). But still, I no longer have any stake in the outcome or the stress that comes with it. But even so, I'm worried.

I'm worried that I might get a phone call tonight from Elizabeth telling me her water broke. Or her contractions are coming every seven minutes, and they *really* hurt. What if I'm sitting between her legs reminding her to take slow deep breaths while eighty potential jurors are sitting in my courtroom waiting for the judge.

I'm worried I'll be delivering a baby when I'm supposed to be in court.

This is why I stopped being a midwife when I became a judge. I just couldn't figure out how to make the schedule work. Since becoming a judge when the phone rings in the middle of the night, it's the police wanting me to approve a search warrant, not a woman thinking she's in labor. I have been relieved that I don't have to be on call for middle of the night labors, but that's about it. Everything else about being a midwife, I have missed.

Then Elizabeth found out she was pregnant. She called and was rambling with excitement:

Since you delivered all my mom's babies I know what it's like to have you as a midwife. I've seen you do everything for my Mom. I know exactly how you work and what it will be like.

Like when my younger brothers and sisters were born. I saw them all.

I remember when Holly was born and you were giving my Mom shots in her leg. You hadn't done that after the other babies. You smiled and said that she was bleeding a little too much, like it was no big deal, but I could tell you were scared.

But I also knew you would fix it.

Well, so, anyway, I always thought that when I had a baby I would want you to be my midwife. I just planned on it. Expected it. All my sisters feel the same way.

And Aiden is SO excited. He's great. You have to meet him.

We were planning to get married even before this.

At first he wasn't sure about a home birth, but I told him all about you and that this is what I wanted and he said it was up to me. That I should decide since I'm the one having the baby.

And I don't want to go to the hospital. I don't want them to take the baby away and give me an IV and all that stuff.

Or have someone I don't know walking in the room while I'm, you know, having the baby. Like with my legs spread. I mean, I already know you and feel comfortable with you and I just couldn't imagine anything else.

I don't want to put you on the spot or anything, and I know you must be really busy, but, so, what I want to know, Sheri, is if you're still being a midwife now that you're a judge? And I really hope so, because I just can't imagine having my baby with anyone else!

Somehow the schedule will work out, I told myself. It always has in the past.

So now I'm worried, like I used to be, that the call will come during the week, when I'm in court and I can't leave. Elizabeth called this morning. Sunday (wouldn't that be great if it happened today because I could still sleep tonight and be in court tomorrow for the jury selection. I could do the follow up appointment with Elizabeth and the baby tomorrow evening, after work). She said she feels like something is "down there" and the contractions that have been coming and going, feel stronger.

I went to her house, sat on the end of her mother's bed, where her brothers and sisters were born, and we talked. She had some mucous come out of her earlier. No blood in it.

I put on a glove, show her the two fingers I'm going to put into her, ask if she's ready, and then examine her. I confirm that the head is very low, low enough that Aiden (who became her husband when I married them a few weeks ago) can feel it when I guide his fingers (WOW—that's really the head?!). She's one centimeter dilated. Could be tonight, could be a week from now. We just have to wait.

She's apologetic for calling me over. I tell her not to worry. I leave after telling her she should call if she feels like something is different. I assure her I really do want to know about any changes.

I was going to spend the day cleaning the house and making lunch to bring to work tomorrow. I'll cook for the whole office—which is four people. The court house is so remote that there are only two restaurants in this small town; a coffee shop with sandwiches, and a Mexican restaurant which describes its food as 'Spanish.' It's impossible for me to go to either restaurant without seeing someone who is in court with me that day. It's awkward and I prefer avoiding the encounters. Anyway, I like seeing my coworkers happy eating the meals I make.

I have planned to make spinach and mushroom quiche, and cranberry-apricot bread for dessert. My bailiff won't like the spinach or the mushrooms (if you can't buy it at the concessions stand at a sports arena, then mostly he doesn't want to eat it), but there is already bread, cheese and sliced turkey at the office. The emergency lunch when someone doesn't like my menu.

I have to buy most of the ingredients for the meal, so on the way home from Elizabeth's house I stop at Wal-Mart, which is the only full sized grocery store in town. When I walk past the deli section I look behind the counter for Claudia, whose baby I delivered a few years ago. Her water never broke and the baby came out still inside the sac. I tore it open with my fingers as he was being born. Folklore says a baby born like that is an Angel. She's not working today. I get what I need and head to the registers.

While I'm waiting in line a man comes up to me. I am wearing jeans, sneakers, and a light green t-shirt. I look like every other weekend shopper at the Espanola Wal-Mart, only I'm not Hispanic. The man is in his twenties, clean clothes, and a short haircut.

He begs my pardon and then asks me if I'll be paying in cash. I ask why he wants to know. He flashes what looks like a credit card but says that it's an EBT card—the modern version of the old food stamps booklet. He wants to turn the balance into cash. He would let me use the card for my groceries, and I would give him the cash. And, as a bonus, he would let me pay him only half the cost. I would get forty dollars worth of groceries by paying him twenty dollars. I tell him I'm not paying with cash and he moves on to the woman in the line next to me.

What I know happened is one of two things: 1) he stole the card, or 2) he sold someone drugs who paid him with the EBT card. As I watch him work the other people in line I consider telling him he really shouldn't be doing that since it's illegal to use the card for anything other than food, and then only by the person it's issued to. For once I decide to mind my own business and try not to think about the kids going hungry so the mom can get her heroin. I look at the cover of *People en Espanol* and silently translate all of the headlines.

After I load the groceries in my car, and am pushing the cart into the cart holder a few spaces away, a young man, maybe twenty, and his girlfriend come up to me. He is wearing a short sleeved t-shirt and dark baggy pants. He's emaciated from drug use. The girlfriend too. I can see the tattoos on his arms, neck and his face. As he gets closer I can read "WSL" tattooed in script next to this right eye. West Side Locos. One of the gangs in town.

"Excuse me, Ma'am" I'm not at all afraid. I have been approached in parking lots for money for years. People from out of town are caught off guard, but those of us who live here have sadly come to expect it.

There's usually a sad story about needing money because a car broke down, or a daughter needs school supplies, or trying to get gas money to get to Santa Fe, or, refreshingly, no excuse but just the request for money. Whatever the story, the money is for drugs. Period.

When this kid approaches me I know what he is going to ask and I know I will say no. I usually try to shorten the whole event and before they can even start talking I say, "I'm not giving you any money for drugs." Today I don't feel rushed.

"Yes?" I say politely like I don't know what he wants.

"Do you have any money you could spare? Me and my girlfriend just need some gas money."

"No. Sorry." I say slowly, shaking my head slightly from side to side. He looks so familiar. He turns and takes a step, scanning the parking lot for the next closest shopper, and then I remember. I call after him, "I think I know you."

He turns back around. "Really?"

"Yeah. From drug court. I think I know you from drug court a few years ago." It comes back to me. He was in the program when he was about fifteen. He was already using heroin. A really sweet kid but came from a whole family of drug users. Mom, grandparents, aunts and uncles, cousins, siblings. Just surrounded by them. There was always someone in the house who was high. His mother had finally cleaned up and was hoping she could get her kids clean. She had a bunch of health problems from her years of use, but was trying. She worked at a bar and was gone all night. Her kids would have their friends over to the house or just go out partying with them. The Mom had lost control years ago.

He tilts his head and focuses on my face, trying to figure out who I am. "I was in drug court," he admits, "but who are you?"

"I'm the judge."

"Sheri? You're Judge Sheri?" He smiles. "How are you?"

"Better than you. I'm not begging for money for a fix." He hangs his head like he's been caught. "You know, if you could keep clean you'd probably be a lot happier."

He speaks quietly. "I know. It's just really hard."

"I know it's hard. But I also know you can do it." I'm not sure I actually believe that. "Well, good luck to you." And I clang my cart into the others and walk towards my car.

Angela. That's it. His mother's name is Angela. I sit in the front seat of my car staring straight ahead and try to remember his name.

The last time I saw him was about two and a half years ago. He'd already been kicked out of drug court, for the second or third time, for non-participation. I was getting gas on the way to work. He came stumbling into the parking lot and called out for me. "Judge Sheri, is that you?" He asked me if I wanted to buy some movies.

He lifted his shirt to reveal five or six square plastic CD cases he had hidden between his waist band and his too thin stomach. His clothes were filthy, his hair was stringy, he had dark circles under his eyes, and generally looked like he had been run over by a truck. I told him I didn't want to buy any stolen CD's. He desperately tried to convince me they weren't stolen (my sister gave them to me because she was moving) and that I should buy one. Only a dollar.

I told him he looked awful and I would get him something to eat in the convenience store. He said that he couldn't eat anything because his teeth were all messed up from the meth he had used for so long, but he would take some coffee.

We walked into the convenience store and the clerk and the other morning customers froze and looked at us. Me in a skirt, gold jewelry, heels, and fresh make-up. And him. We looked like some Halloween version of opposites. He wandered over to the coffee station as people moved back to let him pass. He couldn't figure out how to get the coffee out so I did it for him. He had started sipping it and I went to the register to pay. The clerk waved me off and said not to worry about it. She wanted to get us - him - out of the store.

Outside he asked me for a ride to his cousin's house. He said he had just gotten out of the hospital. He explained that he had overdosed last night and the cops found him on the side of the road and they thought he was dead.

"They called my mom and everything. But I *wasn't* dead!" He tells me triumphantly, "I was just *almost* dead."

They kicked him out of the emergency room this morning and his mom wouldn't even give him a ride. She said she didn't want to see him again until he was clean (good for her!).

"Good for her," I interrupted.

I told him I would give him a ride to the detox center in Taos, but not to his cousin's because I knew he would just get high there.

"No thanks. But hey, could you call my mom and tell her I'm okay?"

"You should call her yourself?"

He just shakes his head and walks off.

Now, looking out of my car window, watching him walk across the Wal-Mart parking lot with his druggie girlfriend, approaching another person for money, I figure every day for him for the last two years has been some mixture of the emergency room, the gas station, and today. If he doesn't get the money he needs, he'll break into someone's house or car and steal something he can sell. Maybe if he's really desperate he'll pull a woman's purse off her arm. If he ends up knocking her down and she gets hurt, he'll feel bad about it, but that's just what happens. Hopefully the woman he chooses won't be holding a baby, like the guy I had in court a few weeks ago.

He's had multiple opportunities for drug treatment and he's rejected all of them. I have finally made peace with the sad realization that this is exactly how he and plenty of others just like him want to live their lives; from fix to fix. My position, power, influence, smarts, and money can't change that.

He'll be dead soon.

On the fifteen minute drive home I replay a conversation I had a few days ago with the head attorney for the public defender's office. He was subtly trying to tell me I needed to give lighter sentences if I wanted to be retained at the next election. I should sentence repeat offenders to treatment. Give them a second chance. Help people get over their addiction instead of locking them up. If they don't want to do go treatment on their own, I should make them. Order them to do it. Force them to get better. That way, the addicts gets clean, stop committing crimes for drug money, and the community is safe. Everyone benefits.

If only it actually worked that way, I think to myself. Thanks for your advice, but I don't think I'll be changing how I do things.

Now, I wonder if I have any ground cumin at home? That would make the quiche just perfect.

www.ingramcontent.com/pod-product-compliance
Lightning Source LLC
Chambersburg PA
CBHW022008080426
42733CB00007B/527